BROTH

SING ON!

CONDUCTING THE
TENOR-BASS CHOIR

ISBN 978-1-4803-2843-3

Hal Leonard Corporation
7777 W. Bluemound Rd.
P.O. Box 13819
Milwaukee, WI 53213

Library of Congress Cataloging-in-Publication Data

Palant, Jonathan.
 Brothers, sing on! : conducting the tenor-bass choir / Jonathan Palant.
   pages cm
 ISBN 978-1-4803-2843-3
1. Choral conducting. 2. Choral singing--Instruction and study. 3. Men's choirs--Instruction and study. I. Title.
 MT85.P34 2014
 782.8'145--dc23
                                 2014029046

Printed in the U.S.A.

Visit Hal Leonard Online at **www.halleonard.com**

BROTHERS, SING ON!

CONDUCTING THE TENOR-BASS CHOIR

BY JONATHAN PALANT
FOREWORD BY ANTON ARMSTRONG

HAL•LEONARD®

WITH COMMENTARY BY:

Steven Albaugh

Christopher Aspaas

Peter Bagley

Christine Bass

Frank Bianchi

Jerry Blackstone

Kerry Brennan

Derrick Brookins

Lesley Childs, M.D.

Dennis Coleman

Karl Dent

Rollo Dilworth

Laura Farnell

Kari Gilbertson

Amy Hamilton

Thomas Jenrette

Jefferson Johnson

Jeremy D. Jones

Diane Loomer

Fernando Malvar-Ruiz

Jameson Marvin

Ted Mau, M.D.

Alan McClung

Kevin Meidl

Francisco Núñez

Matthew Oltman

Paul Rardin

James Rodde

Gary Schwartzhoff

Ethan Sperry

Robert Ward

TABLE OF CONTENTS

Foreword by Anton E. Armstrong..viii

Dedication xi

Introduction..xii

Chapters

    1. A History of Men's Choral Singing 1

    2. Anatomy of the Male Voice 7

    3. The Product: Choral Tone 18

    4. Intonation..25

    5. Parts and Placement..32

    6. The Adolescent Male Voice:
        Categorization to Maturation 39

    7. Programming and Repertoire Selection...65

    8. Auditions...95

    9. Warm-Ups..103

  10. Sight-Singing 114

  11. Recruiting..119

  12. Fund-Raising 129

  13. Travel...136

Appendices

    A. Organizations and Associations 150

    B. Tools for Teaching Sight-Singing...153

    C. Further Reading on Working with Adolescent Male Voices............155

    D. 10 Sample Concert Programs for Male Choirs 156

    E. 50 Recommended Titles for Adolescent Male Choirs 167

    F. 100 Recommended Titles for Male Choirs 171

Biographies of Contributing Authors...179

About the Author..186

FOREWORD

by Anton E. Armstrong, DMA
St. Olaf College

Brothers, Sing On! Conducting the Tenor-Bass Choir by Jonathan Palant is a welcome addition to the choral pedagogy literature addressing the training of male singers. Dr. Palant has compiled a practical monograph that is a comprehensive exploration of the challenges and rewards of working with the evolving adolescent-through-adult male singer. This book reflects Jonathan Palant's considerable experience working with secondary-school-aged singers, collegiate singers, adult church choirs, and fine community choirs such as the highly acclaimed Turtle Creek Chorale. Yet what gives this study added value is his incorporation of the teaching strategies and perspectives of over two dozen seasoned vocal music educators and conductors working with male singers of all ages.

The opening chapter provides an engaging introduction to the seductive power that beautiful choral singing can have on both performer and listener. Dr. Palant and his contributing authors then present a concise historical overview of the tradition of male ensemble singing beginning as far back as ancient Greece, with emphasis on the influential development of male choruses in England and Germany during the eighteenth and nineteenth centuries. His second chapter, "Anatomy of the Male Voice," offers sound and contemporary understanding to the physical workings of the singing voice. The reader is shepherded through this at times complicated information in a clear, accessible way by two knowledgeable otolaryngologists, Dr. Ted Mau and Dr. Lesley Childs, as well as Amy Hamilton, who is a speech language pathologist and certified singing vocologist. In this chapter these three experts, through a scientific lens, answer practical questions regarding the physiology of the voice as well as common concerns regarding vocal health issues. These viewpoints reflect sound scientific/medical information but are offered with the sensitivity of a singer.

As the monograph moves into such areas as vocal technique, tone production, intonation, and terminology for categorizing singers, Dr. Palant not only shares his own pedagogical perspectives, but also brings in the wealth of wisdom and expertise from these more than two dozen vocal music educators. Noteworthy is the focus Dr. Palant gives to the topic of the male evolving/changing voice. His presentation of two of the leading historical teaching strategies as developed by Irvin Cooper and John Cooksey in dealing with the evolving/changing voice is well-done. He precedes the presentation of those two authors' work with some fine current research as to what occurs physiologically during the onset of puberty in the adolescent male singer. Commentary is offered by such gifted pedagogues as Rollo Dilworth, Kevin Meidl, and Francisco Núñez, as well as a host of the other contributors to this volume noted for their work with the unchanged and evolving male singer. The book has helpful, practical suggestions addressed specifically to female music educators who will not have experienced this phenomenon of the evolving/changing voice as their male counterparts may have during their respective adolescent maturation. Yet Dr. Palant has some equally valuable guidelines for male music educators to assist them in working with these singers in vocal transition. Furthermore, between the perspectives presented by Dr. Palant and his noted contributing authors, they also begin to address some of the social/psychological issues that face male singers participating in a choral ensemble.

One will find common as well as distinctive approaches to such topics as vocal placements, vocal warm-ups, singers with limited ranges, pitch-matching issues, choral formation of singers, and selection of repertoire by the many other gifted colleagues who represent years of successful teaching with a wide age range of tenor/bass singers. The focus on the criteria and selection of appropriate literature for male choruses as well as creative programming concepts is given great importance in this book from a variety of perspectives. I appreciated that the emphasis was not just on the aesthetic musical value of the work or on practical issues of range and accessibility, which are of course most important considerations. However, repertoire was also considered for the transformative impact it would have on the singers and potentially on the listener. In this way our choral art can and should strive to serve others through performance of fine choral literature. The recommended repertoire lists in Appendix E and F as well as the sample programs in Appendix D alone are worth the price of the book! The remainder of this monograph addresses essential topics such as effective recruitment strategies, audition procedures, developing music literacy (with an emphasis on sight-singing) in the rehearsal setting, useful hints for travel and touring with your male ensembles, and a myriad of successful fund-raising activities to support choral programs.

This book has come about because of Jonathan Palant's strong sense of personal calling and belief that choral singing can contribute to the development of young men as "whole" people. He understands that singing in a choral ensemble, especially a male chorus, can significantly impact the growth of adolescent boys and help them mature into creative, caring, compassionate adult males of strong character. Jonathan Palant understands this through his own personal conversion due to the compelling power of the choral art and his personal witness to this with the singers he has conducted for so many years. I know *Brothers, Sing On! Conducting the Tenor-Bass Choir* will be a resource I will look forward to sharing with my own students and in future workshops with vocal music educators as we lift up men of all ages in "Body, Mind, Spirit, and Voice!"

Anton E. Armstrong, DMA
Harry R. and Thora H. Tosdal Professor of Music
St. Olaf College
Conductor, The St. Olaf Choir

To those with whom I've sung;

learned;

grown;

shared;

traveled;

loved;

I say,

SING ON! BROTHERS, SING ON!

INTRODUCTION

Throughout my career, I often dreamt of being a conference presenter, festival clinician, and published writer. I never knew, though, what topic I'd present on, to whom I would present it, and finally, who would read whatever it was I wrote. My inner voice kept telling me that whatever I had to say had surely been said many times before by musicians and teachers more talented than I. Such insecurity prevented me from putting the proverbial pen to paper until I realized there was, in fact, no current and available printed manual or textbook on working with men's choruses. It was then that I decided to step out on groundless ground and begin writing down my own thoughts on the subject.

It wasn't long before I recognized a pattern in my approach to writing. Every chapter commenced with a description and outline of my own teaching methodology, followed by an explanation of various techniques I had seen other conductors use in a variety of musical settings. The question then arose—why not ask those other conductors to contribute to my book? If it would be possible to include the opinions, strategies, anecdotes, and vast knowledge of those I have long admired written in their own words, then this is what I would set out to do.

Brothers, Sing On! Conducting the Tenor-Bass Choir is a comprehensive resource guide for conductors of post-pubescent, all-male choirs. Subjects range from creating a beautiful men's choral tone and programming the perfect concert set, to organizational structure and executing a successful fund-raiser. This book addresses a variety of topics not found elsewhere in print.

Every chapter offers practitioner-friendly strategies, practical tools, personal anecdotes, and experiential reflections on working with all-male choirs at both the high school and university levels, as well as with community men's choruses. More than two dozen veteran teacher/conductors, all with significant experience conducting tenor-bass ensembles of various age groups and levels, impart their knowledge on specific, relevant topics.

Chapter introductions are followed by a series of questions and answers specific and applicable to each topic. The answers written by contributing authors begin with his or her name in parentheses. All other answers and comments were written by me.

It is assumed that readers have a basic understanding of choral pedagogy and terminology.

A book such as this does not come to fruition without the generous support, guidance, and patience of many individuals. I am, of course, most grateful to the conductors, educators, and physicians who authored thorough, thoughtful responses to each of my questions.

Their knowledge of and passion for this particular choral genre are displayed throughout this book.

I am indebted to Jamie Rawson and Dulcie Shoener for their proofreading skills and their reliability. To Juan Pimentel, thank you for keeping my cup filled each day I sat working in the corner of your shop. Lastly, I acknowledge Mark Mullaney for being my best friend and greatest champion.

CHAPTER 1
A HISTORY OF MEN'S CHORAL SINGING

MY PERSONAL JOURNEY

My love for choral singing began in a somewhat unusual way. I was a freshman in high school and the piece was Henry Purcell's *Come, Ye Sons of Art*. As a young percussionist, I was experiencing a choral-orchestral work for the first time. I was called upon to play timpani only in the last movement of the nine-movement piece, but Mrs. Peasley, the choir director and conductor, told me in rehearsal she would cue me at the start of the eighth movement. This way I'd be ready for my "triumphal" debut. I had worked on the part in my private lessons, practiced at home endlessly, and felt prepared, yet terribly nervous.

"*Psst!*"

"*PSSSSSSSST!*" My older sister, a senior and a member of the alto section, stood behind me on the risers nodding her head in a somewhat distressed manner. She was signaling me to play. If one had been given, I had missed Mrs. Peasley's cue altogether. I stood up, checked the tuning on the two kettledrums, and began to play something not composed by Purcell. I got to hit the drums a few times before Mrs. Peasley signaled the final note of the piece. I rolled through the fermata and all was over.

I had missed it; I had missed all of it.

Once the tears and feelings of extreme embarrassment subsided, I figured out that I missed my cue, as well as the entire ninth movement for that matter, because I was utterly engrossed in the singing. The chorus was having so much fun! The singers weren't alone behind a thirty-pound instrument or off in a corner with a music stand between themselves and the conductor. Each singer was being fed by the energy of his or her neighbor and by the music they created naturally; it was human music. I hadn't felt that before as a member of the orchestra or band. Not to say it doesn't exist, of course, it just didn't for me at that time.

The next school year, I signed up for both band and choir. I may have missed Mrs. Peasley's cue that day, but not the one that has enriched my life ever since.

TODAY'S GLEE CLUB:
IN TRADITION, CAMARADERIE, AND MUSICAL EXCELLENCE

My sophomore year in college, I joined the University of Michigan Men's Glee Club and, again, my life changed for the better. "In Tradition, Camaraderie, and Musical Excellence" is the Michigan Men's Glee Club motto. As members of the Club, we say it, write it, believe it, and are very proud of it. In college, I wasn't one to pledge a fraternity, participate in intramural sports, or tend to my religious beliefs. Instead, I signed up for Men's Glee Club. The first rehearsal made quite an impression on me. Jerry Blackstone, conductor of the group from 1988 to 2002, had us warming up within minutes of my walking into the rehearsal hall. Incidentally, the rehearsal took place in the same room as my Psychology 101 course earlier that day.

"In your Julia Child voice, please," he instructed, using his own bellowing falsetto. I had never seen or heard a roomful of men hoot in such a way. It was funny to say the least, but over time I learned just how valuable a tool this was—and remains today.

I remember much from my four years in Glee Club, but perhaps nothing more than the sound. I remember our singing in rehearsal and our performances onstage at Ann Arbor's Hill Auditorium, and I remember our sound in magnificent venues such as Buenos Aires' Teatro Colón and Boston's Faneuil Hall. I also recall glorious moments of *fortissimo* singing, as well as the purest of *pianissimo* entrances. No matter where or what we sang, we performed with both passion and compassion.

I had been exposed to all kinds of music throughout my childhood and teen years, and I can't say for certain it was membership in this particular ensemble that motivated me to choose a career in choral music. However, it was in those four years that I discovered my capacity and desire for "tradition, camaraderie, and musical excellence."

"My" Michigan Men's Glee Club can boast many attributes, but being the oldest of its kind is not one of them. The Harvard Glee Club was established in March 1858, a year before Michigan's Club, and is the oldest American collegiate men's chorus in existence today. The chorus, while not the largest in the United States, pioneered many of the traditions others now claim as their own.

The collegiate all-male choir is not the only source for quality male singing, however. Refer to Appendix A for more information on locating a men's chorus in your area.

Historically speaking, community men's choirs can be traced much further back than Harvard and the mid-nineteenth century.

The responses to the following questions were written by Dr. Jeremy D. Jones, director of choral activities, Miami University.

HOW FAR BACK CAN WE TRACE THE HISTORY OF CHOIRS? WHAT IS THE EARLIEST WRITTEN RECORD OF THIS ART FORM?

The origins of choral music are found in traditional music, as opposed to folk music. The oldest unambiguously choral repertory that survives is that of ancient Greece, of which the most complete records are found in the second-century BC Delphic hymns and the second-century AD hymns of Mesomedes.

The earliest notated music of Western Europe is Gregorian chant—named after Pope Gregory I, Bishop of Rome from 590 to 604, who is credited with having ordered the simplification and cataloging of music assigned to specific celebrations in the church calendar. The resulting body of music is the first to be notated in a system ancestral to modern musical notation.

WHAT WAS ENGLAND'S ROLE IN THE HISTORY OF MALE CHORAL SINGING?

English male singing societies were commonly referred to as "catch" or "glee" clubs and were most often informal in nature. Singing societies were a large part of English life. As this movement continued to develop across the nation, membership expanded from the socially elite to include the middle class, as well as professional musicians. While membership and the popularity of male singing societies were on the rise, so too was the musical merit of the compositions they sang. Three musical styles that became popular were the catch, glee, and partsong. The first published books of catches appeared in 1609 by the well-known English composer and theorist Thomas Ravencroft (ca. 1592-ca. 1635). Catches were generally composed in an easy, straightforward manner as rounds. The development of the English glee began to flourish in the mid-eighteenth century. Compared to the catch, glees embodied a more sophisticated compositional approach that wedded poetic ideas to musical motives best capturing the essence of each word and idea. This was the result of a renewed interest in the English madrigal.

The continued development of a loftier musical art form eventually resulted in the partsong, which typified much of the English choral writing by the beginning of the nineteenth century. Partsongs were generally considered to be more technically challenging, longer in duration, and with more musical substance than glees and catches.

The most prominent and versatile composer to have contributed to the form of glees and catches was Samuel Webbe (1740-1816). Webbe composed several hundred catches and glees representing a wide range of topics from the amusing to the serious. He won numerous composition awards, the first in 1766 when he received the first annual prize in the composition contest sponsored by the Catch Club for *O that I had wings*. Important composers who helped cultivate the partsong tradition embedded in the nineteenth century include William Beale (1784-1854), Robert Pearsall (1795-1856), Charles Stanford (1852-1924), and Edward Elgar (1857-1934). As the tradition of partsongs continued into the twentieth century, such composers as Gustav Holst (1874-1934) and Ralph Vaughan Williams (1872-1958) also incorporated folk songs into their compositions.

WHAT ROLE DID GERMAN-SPEAKING COUNTRIES PLAY IN THE DEVELOPMENT OF MEN'S CHOIRS DURING THE NINETEENTH CENTURY?

Although England's position in the formalized structure and elevated musical standards of male choral singing is significant, the most substantial tradition of male singing societies was established in Germany in the early nineteenth century. Carl Zelter (1758-1832) established the first German all-male singing organization in Berlin in 1809 and called it a *Liedertafel*, meaning "song-table." The mission of this organization was similar to those found in England, to encourage original compositions for male voices with musical value. Likewise, Zelter's *Liedertafel* of twenty-five men embraced the earliest traditions of singing societies with eating and drinking. As early as 1815, *Liedertafel* groups began to expand across Germany—in Frankfurt, Magdeburg, Hamburg, Munich, Cologne, Leipzig, and others. They were used to promote fellowship and to encourage the advancement of German song and poetry. As this expansion increased, organizations began to accept a more inclusive membership than the earlier elite groups such as Zelter's. Singing societies with a wider range of membership were referred to as *Liedertafel* groups and the smaller, more selective groups were known as *Liederkranz*, or song cycle. Another important development during the early nineteenth century was the formalization of singing clubs among the German Army ranks. This later led to the inception of glee clubs among German universities, and by the mid-nineteenth century hundreds of university glee clubs had been established. It is also interesting to note that the dramatic increase of male singing groups in German universities is similar to the influx of collegiate glee clubs in the United States after the Civil War (1861-65).

The abundance of male singing societies that developed in the nineteenth century motivated numerous professional musicians to be involved in this artistic movement. Composers were inspired to write in the male choral medium to help advance German song and poetry. By the mid- to late nineteenth century, the *Liedertafel* movement was increasingly characterized by folk-like and patriotic sentiments. Song festivals, known as *Sängerfeste*, were held in an attempt to foster and express nationalistic pride. Some of the more representative composers of the nineteenth-century *Liedertafel* movement include

Franz Schubert (1797-1828), Robert Schumann (1810-56), Felix Mendelssohn (1809-47), Franz Liszt (1811-86), and Anton Bruckner (1824-96). By the end of the nineteenth century the *Liedertafel* movement had evolved from simple partsongs to works with orchestral accompaniment.

WHY DO WE OFTEN CALL THEM GLEE CLUBS?

The identity of male choruses, referred to as glee clubs—especially by many of the collegiate groups in the United States—can be traced back to the early male singing societies in England. A hallmark characteristic of male singing societies in England throughout their early history, during the eighteenth and nineteenth centuries, was the singing of musical styles known as catches and glees. The term "glee" is an Old English word meaning "mirth" or "entertainment." Although the term lends itself to the belief that musical compositions would include only those associated with joy and merriment, composers also wrote glees based on more serious textual ideas. The catch, however, preceded the glee as the most popular musical form and is evidenced as early as the seventeenth century. The catch was commonly known for its witty and often lewd or indecent texts that lauded the pleasurable ideas of drink and sex. One might imagine then that this less-than-profound musical style would have been associated only within the male singing circles, not for a public audience. It was the prominence of these two musical styles inherent in the male singing societies of England that eventually resulted in many singing groups naming themselves catch or glee clubs.

The first group to adopt an official name bearing the term catch was the widely known London-based Noblemen and Gentlemen's Catch Club in 1761. The first named Glee Club formed at the Harrow School, London, England, in 1787 and, unlike the Noblemen and Gentlemen's Catch Club, consisted of a wide-ranging membership that included the middle class. During the mid- to late eighteenth century, many of these groups with informal beginnings advanced to become more formalized groups for the purpose of enhancing the musical and artistic merit of glee compositions. The Noblemen and Gentlemen's Catch Club, for example, sponsored composition competitions in an effort to improve and foster the English tradition of male choral singing. The aforementioned English composer Samuel Webbe is often considered one of the most influential composers in improving this art form, winning numerous composition contests. His most famous glee, *Glorious Apollo*, was composed and dedicated as the theme song of the Glee Club in the year of its official organization. He came to be called the "Prince of Glee Writers" because of his prolific output.

The rich histories associated with the Noblemen and Gentlemen's Catch Club and the Glee Club, and other groups like them, in many respects parallel the development of many American collegiate glee clubs. While a large majority of groups began informally as a means of socialization and relaxation, the artistic desires to further promote the male choral art eventually took precedence while maintaining the strong social presence of their early beginnings.

CHAPTER 2
ANATOMY OF THE MALE VOICE

Definition of PEDAGOGY

: the art, science, profession of teaching; especially: education.[1]

Definition of VOCAL PEDAGOGY

: the study and art of voice instruction and technique.

Many choral conductors have never taken a class in vocal pedagogy. Schools of music frequently require this of their vocal performance majors, but few require it from choral music education and conducting majors. A logical question then arises—are we, as learned conductors, qualified to teach singing techniques to our choristers? Think about it. Would you entrust your choral ensemble to the private or studio voice teacher? Most choral conductors will read that last question and chuckle, because not only have they not thought about it, the answer is likely an emphatic no.

The following paragraph contains pointed questions for comparison purposes only; the word "typical" appears in quotation marks because it is undefinable.

Is the "typical" voice teacher capable of conducting a men's chorus in a Palestrina motet or a Brahms partsong? Does the "typical" voice teacher have enough knowledge of choral tone to balance the tenor and bass sections? What does a voice teacher know about choral diction? That last example, of course, has no merit, as "typical" voice teachers often know a whole lot more about diction than we conductors do. That said, how much does the "typical" choral conductor know about the physiology of human voice production? Do we know how to adequately identify and explain the parts of the larynx and their function? Do we know how to properly teach our students to manipulate vibrato without adversely affecting natural airflow? Do we know why most young men have a hard time singing high F and F-sharp and what exercises are best suited for improving this technique? The answer to many of these questions, when asked of the "typical" choral conductor, is "no."

It is no secret that choral conductors and private voice teachers have long been at odds over what is [believed to be] best for our singers. The choice of repertoire, the selection of soloists, the frequency and length of rehearsals, the use of vibrato, the need to blend voices into a choral setting, the overall section placement (for example, the tenor

---

1 "pedagogy." Merriam-Webster Online Dictionary. Retrieved 2012 from www.merriam-webster.com/dictionary/pedagogy.

who is asked to sing baritone in order for his voice to blend with those around him): these are just a few of the essential decisions that often result in lofty protests lodged against the choral field and, inevitably, its directors.

Many of the objections that voice teachers have with choral conductors and our choral programs are indeed valid, but more often than not, learned conductors can assuage the concerns of most voice teachers simply by demonstrating a thorough understanding of vocal anatomy, voice production and appropriate corrective measures, and a great ability to be flexible both on and off the stage.

With the help of otolaryngologists Dr. Ted Mau and Dr. Lesley Childs, along with speech language pathologist and certified singing vocologist Amy Hamilton, the following pages offer information specific to the male voice and male vocal anatomy.

ARE THEY VOCAL CORDS, CHORDS, OR FOLDS?

It is endearing that singers often refer to the vocal cords or vocal folds as vocal "chords." A chord is a musical term, not an anatomical one. So with that knowledge, why do some people refer to the vocal cords as vocal folds?

When curious doctors of the 1800s began to look down people's throats to figure out what the sound organ looked like, they placed a little mirror on a stick and positioned the mirror in the back of the mouth. They shined a beam of light on the mirror as the patient made a sound. What they saw appeared to be two white cords coming together and vibrating; that's why the vocal cords received the name by which they are still commonly known to this day. However, voice scientists have known since the 1970s that each simple-looking cord actually consists of a layered structure with each layer playing a unique role in voice production. Most laryngologists and voice scientists therefore refer to "vocal cords" as "vocal folds" to do justice to the intricate, fine structure of the voice organ.

HOW DOES A MAN'S VOCAL ANATOMY DIFFER FROM THAT OF A WOMAN'S?

Refer to Figures 1 and 2.

Even in this enlightened age of gender equality, great differences remain between female and male vocal anatomies. On average, men have much larger larynges (the plural form of *larynx*). As a result, male vocal folds are 40 to 60 percent longer than female vocal folds. This difference alone largely accounts for the typically deeper male voice and the higher female voice. Male vocal folds are also thicker, which adds to the pitch difference. Piano strings, for example, are similar to vocal folds in that the lower-pitched strings are not only longer than the higher-pitched ones, but they are significantly thicker as well. In addition, the fine structure of the vocal folds also differs between the genders. While women and men share the same vocal fold layer architecture, the content of molecules that make up the layers differs somewhat, so that female and male vocal folds have slightly different vibratory properties. Some voice scientists speculate that this difference may partly explain why women are more prone to getting vocal fold nodules.

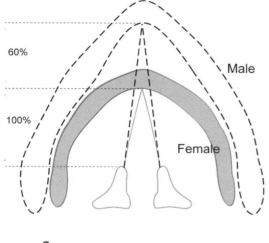

FIGURE 1

In this aerial view of the laryngeal structure, the dashed line outlining the shape (in the male) and the solid outlined shape (in the female) both represent the thyroid cartilage, which "houses" the vocal folds. The knob-like structures at the back of the voice box (bottom of the picture) are representative of the arytenoid cartilages, which rotate the vocal folds in and out. The vocal folds are indicated by the upside-down-V-shaped dashed and gray lines, respectively, in the middle of the diagram.

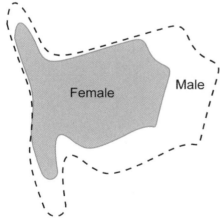

FIGURE 2

Side view of the thyroid cartilage.

WHAT HAPPENS WHEN OUR VOICES "CRACK"?

The smoothness of a voice is rooted in how "periodic" the vocal folds vibrate. At middle C, the vocal folds vibrate about 262 times a second. The two vocal folds come together and come apart in a regular cycle of contact and de-contact that is repeated over and over again. If the vibrations stop for even a fraction of a second, our ears (and our brains, which actually process the sound) hear a crack, or interruption in the sound. This could be caused by a variety of things: a drop of thick mucus that suddenly gets caught between the vocal folds, or sudden tightness of the vocal fold muscles, etc. Most familiar to relatively untrained male singers is the voice crack between the head voice and the falsetto register. Here, during the transition, the vocal folds are held under too much tension to vibrate.

WHAT IS FALSETTO?

Falsetto is a specific register in the male voice. Registers in this instance are loosely defined as distinct regions of voice quality that can be maintained over some ranges of pitch and loudness, according to Dr. Ingo Titze[2].

Typical male speaking registers are called pulse, modal (Refer to Figure 3), and falsetto (Refer to Figure 4). The modal register is what men typically use for most speaking and singing. The falsetto register lies above the modal register in pitch, but the difference extends beyond a simple pitch difference. The male falsetto register is "lighter" in quality. To produce falsetto, the vocal folds actually work a little differently than they do in modal register. In modal register, the vocal folds vibrate against each other. They are not under a significant amount of tension, so a thicker layer of tissue participates in vibration.

In falsetto, the vocal folds are stretched so that they are under more tension. This allows only the superficial part of the vocal folds to vibrate, and they do so at higher frequencies; that is, we perceive a higher pitch. In this register, the vocal folds actually make much less contact with each other compared to modal register.

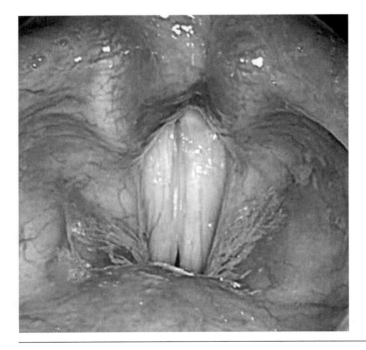

FIGURE 3
Modal voice: the folds are thick, are not stretched, and are fully adducted (touching).

2 Titze, Ingo. *Principles of Voice Production*. National Center for Voice and Speech, Utah: 2000.

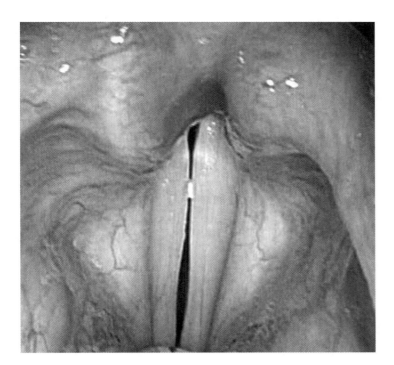

FIGURE 4
Falsetto: the folds are stretched long, are thinner, and are more streamlined in appearance. While barely so, the folds are abducted (not touching).

WHY IS MY VOICE DEEPER THAN USUAL WHEN I WAKE UP IN THE MORNING?

Doctors are not sure if there is a definitive answer to this question based on sound scientific research. However, based on what we know from research and human physiology, we think the following is the most likely explanation.

A good night's sleep results in a slight swelling of the vocal folds. This happens because fluid pressure in the vocal fold circulation is higher when the vocal folds are on the same horizontal level as the heart; that is, when the singer is lying down and the head is parallel with the heart. The pitch or frequency of a vibrating mass goes down as the mass increases. As a result, the little bit of extra fluid in the vocal folds in the morning makes all our voices sound a little lower. After a few hours of being upright, however, the tissue re-equilibrates and the singer starts sounding normal again.

I AM A MAN, BUT MY VOICE IS HIGH AND ALMOST FEMININE-SOUNDING. WHY?

The gender identity of voice quality goes beyond pitch. The fundamental frequency that determines a man's speaking voice is based on one's vocal fold anatomy. A singer with a higher frequency of vibration may be classified as a tenor; however, very few of them would or should be labeled as feminine. To create the impression of a feminine voice, a man's pitch has to be higher than the male average, and the pattern of intonation and inflection in speech would have to mimic that of the typical female.

For men concerned about a feminine-sounding voice, the first step is to talk to a voice specialist. In most cases, they will find that their fundamental speaking frequency is well within the male range. The next step is to work with a voice therapist with expertise in this particular area to identify features of their speech that impart a feminine impression and to learn ways to change them if so desired.

WHAT ARE NODULES AND HOW DO I KNOW IF I HAVE THEM?

Nodules are small bumps on the edge of the vocal folds that develop in response to misuse, overuse, and abuse. (See Figures 5 and 6.) They are similar to a callus in that they represent a firm, thickened area. They come in pairs (one on each fold) and are located at the midpoint of the vocal folds, where the amplitude of the vibration is greatest. When the vocal folds come together during phonation, only the nodules strike together instead of the entire length of the vocal folds, giving the vocal fold aperture a resemblance to an hourglass. Because these nodules prevent complete closure of the folds, a breathy and rough voice results. Fortunately, with speech therapy and improved vocal hygiene, these will often soften and disappear without the need for any surgery.

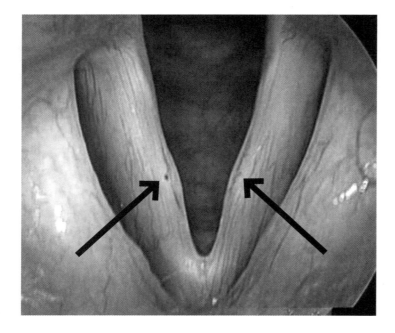

FIGURE 5
Lesions, or protrustions, are noticeable on the front side of each fold in their abducted, or non-phonating, state.

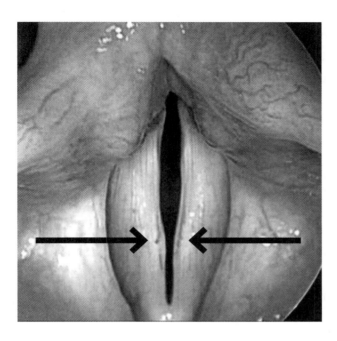

FIGURE 6
Lesions are clearly noticeable when the vocals folds are adducted—in use.

WHY DO INEXPERIENCED MALE SINGERS OFTEN TILT THEIR CHINS UPWARD WHEN TRYING TO SING IN THE HIGHER REGISTER?

Many singers, especially young singers, attempt to muscle their way up to produce higher pitches. They rely heavily on use of the neck musculature when singing in the upper range. The physical movement of lifting the chin when reaching for a higher pitch parallels the perceptual movement of the pitch, just as lowering the chin is often seen to produce lower notes. With excessive head movement or positioning, either the strap muscles (located in the front of the neck) or the paraspinal muscles (in the back of the neck) are engaged and under unnecessary tension. These muscles naturally move with breathing, but should not be under any strain during singing. This excessive muscular effort, if done habitually, can be damaging to the voice. Optimal alignment should have the ears positioned over the shoulders with the chin in a neutral position, neither raised nor lowered. This alignment should be present throughout the entire singing range.

MY NECK HURTS WHEN I'M SINGING. WHAT AM I DOING WRONG?

You should never feel discomfort in your throat or neck with any type of voice use. However, it is very common for people to unconsciously involve neck and throat musculature when singing and even speaking. The end result of any sort of vocal strain is elevation of the larynx in the neck. The muscles that cause this are commonly referred to as the straps in the front of the neck. This unnatural elevation of the larynx will pinch off the sound. Shallow breathing that is higher in the chest can also lead to tension in the neck and throat muscles. Singing with diaphragmatic breath support and optimal postural alignment should decrease excessive neck and throat tension. Singing lessons and voice therapy are often recommended for those with persistent neck discomfort related to voice use.

I HAVE AN UNUSUALLY SOFT SINGING VOICE. WHY?

Every voice should be able to produce a range of dynamics, including normal and louder volumes. A voice that is properly supported using correct technique should produce such effects. Those who cannot or who fear there is something medically or physically wrong should see a laryngologist for a videostrobe exam. Soft or muffled voices often indicate incomplete glottic closure (when the vocal folds do not touch completely when vibrating), which can cause decreased volume with appropriate forward tone focus. Possible causes of incomplete glottic closure include decreased range of motion of a vocal fold, excessive laryngeal muscular effort upon voicing, or a lesion on the vocal fold.

WHAT CLUES MIGHT INDICATE VOCAL POLYPS, NODULES, OR OTHER MEDICALLY TREATABLE PROBLEMS?

Symptoms such as hoarseness, a decrease in vocal range, or throat discomfort that persists more than three to four weeks should prompt a singer to contact a laryngologist. If the voice change is present while both singing and speaking, there may be a lesion or other abnormality on the vocal fold itself. If the difficulty arises only with singing, there may be a behavioral or technical component underlying the change. Ideally, singers in advanced study will have established a relationship with a laryngologist so that a baseline exam can be performed and on file in the case of a vocal change.

WHAT IS LARYNGITIS?

Laryngitis technically means "inflammation of the larynx" or voice box. Frequently, this is caused by an upper respiratory infection, which is most commonly viral and not caused by a bacterial infection. More specifically, when someone has laryngitis, the vocal folds become swollen and have an irritated appearance. Because of this tissue change at the level of the vocal folds, they are significantly more vulnerable to injury. It is important to rest the voice to avoid permanent damage. If the laryngitis does not respond to symptomatic treatment (in the form of increased hydration and voice rest) within two to three weeks, a visit to a local doctor or laryngologist may be necessary. The vocal folds cannot be viewed in a mirror, but instead require a laryngoscopy (a procedure using a medical scope to view the vocal folds) to be performed in a laryngologist's clinic.

I'VE HEARD THAT LEMONS AND HONEY HELP MY SINGING VOICE. IS THIS TRUE?

Lemons and honey are natural remedies that may help to soothe the throat. These and similar remedies are useful in terms of symptom control but do not have any biologic effect on the bacteria responsible for the infection.

Drinking water and inhaling steam to increase both internal and external moisture are more effective than either lemons or honey. In terms of vocal hygiene, dryness and dehydration are the enemy—especially while trying to heal from laryngitis.

HOW MUCH WATER SHOULD I CONSUME FOR MY VOCAL FOLDS TO BE HYDRATED? DO CAFFEINE AND ALCOHOL AFFECT MY SINGING VOICE?

Hydration is imperative for healthy vocal folds. The general rule is to drink 64 ounces of water per day and to limit caffeine and alcohol. For every ounce of caffeine or alcohol consumed, add an equal amount of water, ounce for ounce, to compensate for the drying effects. Plain water is the most beneficial for hydration, but any noncaffeinated beverage can be included in the daily water intake. Although not researched, it is often recommended that singers eat a "wet snack" one hour before a performance. Examples of a wet snack include apples, grapes, watermelon, etc. The action of chewing relaxes the laryngeal musculature and the wetness of the snack is thought to add hydration to the throat.

I WANT TO BE A PROFESSIONAL SINGER. SHOULD I AVOID ANY PHYSICAL ACTIVITIES SUCH AS WEIGHT LIFTING?

Physical activity is okay so long as no breath holding, grunting, excessive engagement of neck musculature, or other vocally abusive behaviors are involved. For example, tennis players tend to grunt loudly when making contact with the ball. This can be vocally damaging with repetition. Diaphragmatic breathing and correct postural alignment should be utilized during any physical activity.

Weight lifting can have an adverse effect on your voice if done incorrectly. You should inhale slowly through your nose on the preparation phase of the motion and exhale through puckered lips on the exertion phase. In other words, you should exhale while lifting the weight. When exhaling, the airflow should be focused at the lips and not at the throat. Breath holding between inhalation and exhalation causes excessive throat tightness. Abdominal-strengthening exercises, such as crunches, should be done while keeping the neck muscles relaxed. Make sure only the abdominal wall is engaged, and not the neck muscles, while performing the exercise.

FROM A DOCTOR'S PERSPECTIVE, WHAT SHOULD I, AS A TEACHER, INCORPORATE INTO MY DAILY WARM-UPS?

Most importantly, these should indeed be *daily*. Even on days we only speak and don't sing, warm-ups are critical and beneficial in order to help avoid vocal strain and possible injury. Warm-ups should represent a gradual increase in vocal demand and should emphasize those exercises that engage one's breath support, release tension in the neck, and focus the placement of sound in an optimal resonating location for our individual sound. After warming up, singers should not be exhausted, but rather energized and primed for excellent vocal technique.

WHAT CHANGES HAPPEN AFTER PUBERTY? AT 20 YEARS OLD, 40 YEARS OLD, 60 YEARS OLD…

According to Richard Miller[3], vocal development continues throughout the fourth decade. College-age voices are thought to be relatively young voices. And, although chronological age is not necessarily a reliable predictor of vocal maturity, voices are thought to be mature when the singer reaches his or her late 20s or early 30s. As we age, our vocal folds begin to lose elasticity and the muscle bulk begins to atrophy and weaken, resulting in vocal fold bowing. As a result, older voices can sound weakened and breathy. One common treatment for vocal fold atrophy is injection augmentation. These injections involve placing a gel-like material into the muscle that makes up the vocal fold, in order to return it to its former shape and size. Laryngologists, either in the office or in the operating room, perform such injection augmentation procedures.

For more information on physical changes during puberty, refer to the chapter titled "The Adolescent Male Voice: Categorization to Maturation."

WHAT ARE THE BEST WAYS TO PROTECT MY VOICE?

To put it simply, overuse, misuse, and abuse are the most common ways people harm their voices. Biologically, the vocal folds are uniquely different from tissues found elsewhere in the body because of the continuous mechanical forces acting on the tissue during vibration. Nowhere else does vibration occur naturally and regularly at frequencies of 100 to 1,000 hertz. It has been proposed that vocal fold tissues may have evolved by developing

---

3 Miller, Richard. The Structure of Singing: System and Art in Vocal Technique. G. Schirmer Books: 1986.

specialized functions to withstand such mechanical stress. Nonetheless, vocal hygiene and preserving one's instrument are of utmost importance! Miller writes, "The most perfect vocal technique cannot surmount some of the demands of the current professional performance world."

Some of the stressors on singers include environmental ones, such as exposure to cigarette smoke, excessive talking prior to performance, and the rigorous demands placed upon both amateur and accomplished artists. Also, the voice is vulnerable to reflux, muscle tension, and upper respiratory infections. Remember, the human voice is an instrument that cannot be traded in or upgraded.

What is vibrato? At what age should I begin to have it?

Vibrato is defined as "a slightly tremulous effect imparted to vocal or instrumental tone for added warmth and expressiveness by slight and rapid variations in pitch."[4] The rate of vibrato typically ranges from four to twelve oscillations per second with an average pitch variant of a semitone, that is, one half step or 100 cents. One theory on vibrato is that it serves as a relaxant principle. When the voice is relaxed, vibrato appears spontaneously and naturally. Although there is variation, vibrato often first becomes apparent in the early teenage years. Every singer should be able to produce vibrato. Often a lack of ability to produce vibrato indicates excessive muscular effort with singing (although it is possible to produce a healthy straight tone). Vibrato is often thought to help optimize vocal fold vibration because of the relaxing principle and balance between airflow and phonation.

My conductor wants me to sing with a straight tone using absolutely no vibrato. Is this healthy?

Constantly singing in a straight tone may cause excess strain, especially on sustained notes at the extremes of range. However, with proper breath support and a tension-free larynx, healthy straight-tone singing is possible. Producing a straight tone in a healthy way requires skill and knowledge of the technique. One's conductor or voice teacher should be consulted for proper instruction.

---

4 "vibrato." Merriam-Webster Online Dictionary. Retrieved 2012 from www.merriam-webster.com/dictionary/vibrato.

CHAPTER 3
THE PRODUCT: CHORAL TONE

A chorus's tone quality, or product, is the sum of many factors. A conductor trained in the English boy choir tradition has a very different concept of choral tone from that of the conservatory-trained opera singer turned chorus conductor, and both of these musicians will have a hugely different concept of sound than the St. Olaf College graduate or past member of the Luther College Nordic Choir. Musical background, vocal training, and ensemble experience often form the basis for one's tastes in choral tone, as well as one's ability to mold it.

Building and shaping tone quality in a men's choir is not dissimilar to doing so with a mixed choir. Basic principles remain the same; however, men have three specific areas that typically require special attention. In my own rehearsals, I often compare the sound of the male voice with that of the cello. Let me explain.

1. **Falsetto.** Use it freely and often, but approach it with great delicacy. Hear the note before you sing, just as a cellist places his or her fingers carefully on the fingerboard and in the exact place before running the bow across the string. Then, with proper support and intention, begin to phonate. Without intention and breath, the falsetto "false starts," resulting in a lack of sound followed by a *pop* when the folds fully engage. A misplaced finger on the fingerboard or bow that isn't properly weighted upon attack will have similar unfortunate results in sound production.

2. **Vocal Fry.** Young singers (and many not-so-young singers) force low notes by adding extra muscle to the sound. Few second tenors are truly able to beautifully sing B2, the second line on the bass clef, yet most love the opportunity during warm-ups to show off how low they think they can go. Imagine a cellist digging into the C string, the lowest string, with the bow. As the bow nears the frog, too much pressure results in a harsh, grinding, dreadful sound. For vocalists, the proper way to approach these notes is to do the exact opposite of digging into the sound. I often ask singers to imagine a hot air balloon landing on the note. All aspects of production remain afloat while the tone, like the hot air balloon, simply touches down. Descending five-note scales that decrescendo are an ideal way to practice this technique. Pick any neutral syllable or combination of syllables. I typically use *loo-aw* [lu:a] beginning in E-flat major.

Repeat descending by half steps

loo - aw,   loo - aw,   loo - aw,   loo - aw,   loo - aw. ___

Descend past the point where singers can sing comfortably. I go beyond only because it is fun and becomes a competition for whoever can sing the lowest note—beautifully or not. Fun is always good, and this is especially so in a men's chorus, but you should remind singers often of the proper techniques needed to create a gorgeous product!

3. **Crossing the Break**. It is rare to find a singer whose falsetto is naturally louder than his modal (chest) voice. Melodic lines that cross the vocal passaggio, the point at which the falsetto meets the modal voice, require the singer to flip between registers and thus adjust the singing dynamic as well.

    For example (see figure below), a baritone melody leaping downward from F, quite high in the full voice male register, to A requires the singer to make several physical and musical adjustments in order to maintain linear beauty. The high F will be most comfortable to sing using the falsetto voice, while the A is most definitely a modal voice pitch. If both registers are employed, the singer will be forced to temper the dynamic contrast between the lighter falsetto note and the weightier sound of the chest voice.

Training inexperienced singers to temper these contrasting registers is vitally important. The cello analogy here is more a visual one than an actual one, but I find when a singer visualizes a cellist's left hand shifting from high on the fingerboard to low on the fingerboard, the singer understands how technically accurate this adjustment needs to be. The left hand moves quickly and smoothly up and down, yet the musical line is not interrupted so long as the bow remains constant. I recommend using a variety of musical excerpts, preferably from your current repertoire, to practice this technique.

Creating our desired choral tone is much more than a few mechanical explanations and a few warm-up exercises. No matter what the makeup of your ensemble, tone preference should be determined by the repertoire itself. Schubert's *Die Nacht* (arranged for TTBB choir by John Leavitt, Hal Leonard Corporation 1943463) deserves a very different concept of sound production than Thomas Tallis' *If Ye Love Me* (Public Domain), yet professionals in our field often assign words like *bright, forward, covered, swallowed,* and my all-time favorite, *dark,* to describe the overall sound of an ensemble. A more accurate and appropriate method is to apply, in combination, these adjectives to each and every vowel sung by the ensemble.

Take the *Ave Maria* text, for example, and consider the production and shape of the first two syllables—*A* and *VE*. How round is the [a] vowel? Is it closer to *aw* or *ah*? Is the jaw dropped or is the mouth more elliptical in shape? For the second vowel, is it a closed [e], an open one, or the all-too-common diphthong? How unified are both these vowels—whatever their intended shape?

Geography also plays a role in developing and manipulating choral tone. Having lived many years in Michigan, I fondly remember the struggle many singers had with the [a] vowel. For singers who speak in this Midwest accent, the sung [a] vowel originates high in the nasal cavity and migrates forward, creating a diphthong from *eh* to *ah*. For example, my own surname, Palant, rhymes with talent. In Michigan, however, it is often pronounced [peh:ah-lent]. Instructing a singer to darken a singular vowel has little effect on making it purer or more aligned with those around him. In my own singing, when a conductor tells me to darken a particular vowel, I most often and inadvertently move the vowel back and down my throat away from the lifted soft palate. Of course, this results in a swallowed sound rather than the desired darkened one. Ultimately, the words we most often associate with choral tone (bright, dark, etc.) have little to do with molding and creating the preferred choral tone. Rather, influencing an ensemble's choral tone is dependent upon our ability, as conductor/teacher, to guide singers through a series of steps hoping they produce a sound that is properly supported, resonant, in tune, and with unified vowels both within their own section and throughout the entire ensemble.

WHEN WORKING WITH A MEN'S CHORUS, WHAT IS YOUR CONCEPT OF CHORAL TONE? WHAT KEY ELEMENTS DO YOU WANT TO HEAR?

(Christopher Aspaas) My concept of choral tone: healthy, free, and exciting.

I remember my first experience as a singer in a male chorus. It was my freshman year in the St. Olaf College Viking Chorus. I was one of about seventy members in this ensemble of eighteen- and nineteen-year-old college men. Robert Scholz (a.k.a. Dr. Bob) stood us up, stretched us out, and immediately started us singing on high C: *Poo poo poo poo poo...* descending from *sol* to *do* in F major with lots of "spooky *oo*" in the tone. That was it—the concept was loud and clear to me—lyric and from the top down.

I have told many of my singers and colleagues that Robert Scholz had the greatest impact on my concept of choral tone, and that remains true to this day. At the core of this ideal is healthy and free singing. Without access to the head voice, this task is insurmountable. Asking, and sometimes forcing, singers to bring their most lyric, connected tone down into their middle register through the *passaggio* helped me to engage male singers in exciting repertoire with a uniform tone and uniform concept of vocal production, all the while maintaining excellent intonation.

Lyricism and vocal drama are perhaps best explained and detailed by Alan Zabriskie in a recent publication by USingersPublishers and editor Kevin Fenton: *Foundations of Choral Tone: A Proactive and Healthy Approach to Vocal Technique and Choral Tone*. In this very accessible text that includes great exercises, diagrams, and lesson-planning tools, Alan shares some fantastic ideas regarding the use of *chiaroscuro*, which is the balance between *chiaro* (bright and forward) and *oscuro* (dark and toward the back) in order to achieve a healthy, open, and resonant tone. By focusing the resonance between these two places, where the male voice tends to get caught, we find a release that is sustainable.

"BLEND" IS OFTEN A TRIGGER WORD FOR CONDUCTORS. WHAT IS YOUR RESPONSE TO THIS? WHAT TECHNIQUES DO YOU FIND MOST EFFECTIVE FOR CREATING A UNIFIED SOUND IN A SMALL ENSEMBLE SETTING?

(Matthew Oltman) The biggest factors that affect blend are vowel uniformity, matching tone color, and accuracy of pitch. In a small ensemble, singers should be encouraged to discuss vowel shapes and to develop a language to express their ideas. The International Phonetic Alphabet is useful in this endeavor so long as the ensemble agrees on the sound of each symbol. Take the open E vowel, for example. Where you are from dictates how open this vowel will actually sound. This varies considerably! Singers should also pay attention to the mouths of their colleagues, ensuring that each vowel is created in the same way and that each diphthong or triphthong (such as *hour* [aʊər] or *fire* [faɪər]) is executed simultaneously. Tone color needs to be addressed and decided upon based on the needs of the music. Renaissance polyphony often requires a more pure tone with fewer individual characteristics so that each interweaving line sounds like a single voice. Music with complex harmonies might require similar production so that the various-sounding intervals are not obscured. On the other hand, many styles of music are well-served by fuller tone color with more individual characteristics. This way of singing can actually make a small ensemble sound larger than it is and can be quite impressive if it is appropriate to the music. Finally, pitch accuracy and intervallic tuning are essential for an ensemble to blend. Sometimes singers think that pitch accuracy (that is, not being sharp or flat in relation to the other sounding pitches) is a vocal issue. Singers are often seen raising their eyebrows unnaturally and craning their necks in order to "fix" being flat or tucking in their chins and tilting their heads in toward their sternums order to correct being sharp. These are pointless rectifications and usually cause all manner of other vocal problems. The true parts of the body that affect pitch accuracy are the ears, not the vocal cords. Singers in a small ensemble need to learn to hear how their voice "rings" with respect to the other singers in the ensemble. With practice, a singer will hear the vibrations (or lack thereof) that are associated with being in tune. These vibrations will differ depending on where the singer is in his range and on what vowel he is singing.

DO YOU STRIVE FOR CONSISTENCY IN CHORAL TONE?

(Dennis Coleman) Choral tone is determined by the needs of the specific repertoire. I do not want my chorus to sound the same on Brahms as it does on a Broadway tune. Within the classical repertoire, I strive for a round, slightly covered tone that maintains a clear point of resonance necessary for good intonation. I avoid a forced, shouting sound and prefer a buoyant, quiet energy. I also prefer the overall sound to be slightly bottom heavy with more cover in the tone as the range goes higher. For pop music, the chorus is quick to adopt a brighter, more forward tone that supports the text and style. The challenge lies in being able to switch back and forth between these two extremes at will, and often in a single concert.

WHAT IS THE "POINT AND DOME" TECHNIQUE?

(Paul Rardin) A student of mine used this phrase once when describing the men's sound of a terrific professional choir. In a nutshell, Point and Dome allow us to have our timbral cake and eat it too: we get both brightness and warmth in every note.

Point refers to focus in the tone, which gives the sound a sense of being vibrant, resonant, and alive. We achieve Point by focusing our sound toward the "mask" area of the face (think of the acoustics of wood or stone versus carpet) while singing. Some ways of doing this in rehearsal:

- Hold your index finger in front of your mouth about an inch; as you sing a note, move the finger slowly away from your mouth and have your tone "follow" your finger.

- Hold your hands by the side of your head, pointing upward and slightly inward; as you sing a tone, move your hands forward and upward to meet each other, forming a peak above and in front of your face.

- Imagine the tone resonating behind your eyes—or, if you want even brighter sound, behind your teeth.

Dome refers to height and space in the tone, which gives the sound a sense of warmth, richness, and depth. We achieve Dome by maintaining a tall space inside our mouths, no matter the vowel. Some ways of doing this include:

- Pulling imaginary taffy north-south in front of our mouths on each vowel; a five-note warm-up could include *nee-neh-nah-naw-noo*.

- Place the backs of your fingers on your cheeks and glide your fingers upward (coaxing your mouth into a tall position) on each vowel.

WHAT TECHNIQUES DO YOU USE TO CREATE THE CHORAL TONE YOU DESIRE?

(Peter Bagley) There is no one technique, but rather an approach of intense listening and concentration within the confines of the repertoire. Most important is a healthy sound above any or all considerations. Flexibility of the vocal sound within the context of the other singers in each voice part would be the next priority.

"In unison" is the mantra I hold up for all choristers in the ensemble whether it consists of mixed voices or is gender-specific. Consequently, constant listening to each other is the ultimate goal within the rehearsal. I avoid the word "blend" as a specific goal. Paraphrasing the late Robert Shaw, "If everyone is singing the same vowel at the same time, at the same volume, and with the same intensity, the 'blend' is most certainly an achievable goal."

HOW MIGHT YOU DESCRIBE YOUR IDEAL CHORAL TONE?

(Karl Dent) In the ideal, the best choral tone to achieve is one that allows the greatest variety of freedoms, colors, and vocal applications. The men should learn to sing comfortably at every dynamic. If technical freedom is being achieved, the group will find its own color and choral tone. My ideal choral tone is a vertical, forward, effortless sound that is grounded in good breathing and support systems. Descriptive word sets, such as "bright & dark," "forward & tall," "free & responsive," represent my vocabulary. In this age group (collegiate freshmen and sophomores, primarily), my techniques are applied to coordinate all levels of freedom in singing.

FALSETTO IS INTEGRAL TO BEAUTIFUL CHORAL TONE. EXPLAIN THE PURPOSE FALSETTO SERVES IN THE TTBB CHOIR.

(Matthew Oltman) Any adult male who has ever shouted "woo-hoo" at a sporting event has used his falsetto.

(Refer to the chapter titled "Anatomy of the Male Voice" for more information on falsetto production.)

Falsetto is a natural part of the adult male voice that can be trained and developed just like the modal or "chest" voice. In the all-male, professional vocal ensemble Chanticleer, we combine male singers singing in falsetto voice (usually called countertenors, falsettists, or sopranists) with male singers singing in modal voice to create a unique homogeneous sound that differs sonically from an ensemble that mixes male and female voices. Both, however, sing SATB repertoire! This is a bit like a viol consort where the instruments have the same shape and the same timbre and tone quality, but their differing sizes give each instrument its own range. In the same way, an ensemble utilizing the entire spectrum of the male voice from countertenor to bass consists of many different sizes of the same "instrument," in this case, the vocal cords. The likeness of instruments (all male in this case) allows for a different sort of blend than that which is achieved in a mixed ensemble.

(Refer to the chapter titled "Warm-Ups" for exercises targeting the falsetto range.)

CHAPTER 4
INTONATION

I remember well attending a choral symposium in the late 1990s headlined by Dr. Jameson Marvin from Harvard University. The lecture was on tuning. I sat in amazement as the clinician demonstrated various techniques to tune chords no one else in the room heard as being out of tune. Subtle conducting motions, precise verbal instruction, and penetrating eyes prompted the ensemble to alter pitch ever so slightly up or down, creating a sublime sound. Aside from his intense concentration and obvious brilliance, I remember Jim having an absolute command of pitch tendencies and the overtone structure. He made comments such as, "Sing the E ever so softly above the C and not only will the octave resonate, but we'll all hear the fifth above that note too." In all honesty, I didn't hear the fifth above the octave, but I did retain the importance of understanding the harmonic overtone series and how it directly affects choral tone.

The following responses are written by Dr. Jameson Marvin, director of choral activities emeritus, Harvard University.

INTONATION IS A PROBLEM IN MY ENSEMBLE. SOME SECTIONS ALWAYS GO FLAT NO MATTER WHAT I SAY OR DO.

In my experience, tenors flat more than basses because considerable fatigue can accumulate when singing in high ranges or tessituras.

In mixed choirs, I find the following:

- Sopranos go sharp.

- Altos are inaudible.

- Tenors go flat.

- Basses are slow.

In men's choruses, I find the following:

- First tenors go both flat and sharp depending on range, tessitura, dynamic, vowel, and whether they are singing in their falsettos or not.

- Second tenors go flat and are sometimes inaudible.

- Baritones are somewhat slow; it is difficult to hear their internal part at times, causing ear-to-voice pitch problems.

- Basses are definitely very slow and sometimes go flat; there is not great ear-to-voice clarity in the low range. When I say "slow" I am referring to baritone and bass voices moving slowly, resulting in the slowing of the rhythm.

WHAT IS INTONATION?

Unifying pitch—singing with good intonation—is one of the most elusive challenges in the choral art. When a choir sings in tune, the listener is allowed to hear more clearly the music's structural components: harmony, melody, rhythm, and texture. Thus, singing in tune heightens the awareness of structure, which facilitates communication.

A great many factors affect the achievement of good pitch. A choir will not truly sing in tune until its composite vocal sound achieves a unity of timbre. Pitch and timbre together define intonation. The vowels, as well as the pitch, must be tuned. When vowels are matched, the pitch can be unified.

Singing in tune requires good ears and consistent reinforcement by both the conductor and the singer. The responsibility for maintaining good pitch lies ultimately with the singer. While the conductor can provide a singer or ensemble with an initial pitch, or what I call the "pitch standard," acquiring good pitch perception is integrally connected to understanding the process by which it is attained. By teaching choral singers to become conscious of the process by which they individually used to attain the conductor's pitch standard, the responsibility is placed squarely on their shoulders. Once this process becomes clear, choir singers are invigorated by the thinking that is required to re-create good pitch each time, and are stimulated by their own abilities (with friendly conductorial prods) to maintain it.

The better the conductor's ear, the more effectively the conductor's conception of the music (mental-aural image-mind's ear) can be taught to the choir. The ear gathers every bit of information. The information received can be categorized by the four elements that comprise music: duration, pitch, timbre, and intensity. Each element contributes to the composite picture of the whole. The ear has the capacity to hear all four elements at the same time. The mind has the ability to focus selectively on one at a time and also the capacity to assimilate information on all levels simultaneously.

Learning to hear simultaneously on four levels requires natural aptitude, training, and experience. Each rehearsal presents a fresh opportunity to expand the ear's capacities. Concentration is the key. Conductors who possess the capacity to concentrate will reap the rewards of increased auditory perception, and will thus be able to quickly identify information related to duration, pitch, timbre, and intensity. As the ear improves, the conductor's ability to evaluate this information will be greatly enhanced, providing him/her with the knowledge necessary to implement change.

HOW DO YOU LISTEN FOR PITCH ACCURACY?

Picture a dial. While the choir is singing, slowly turn the dial and focus your concentration on one element of music at a time. Spend considerable time listening to one element— *pitch*, for example, or quality, amplitude, accuracy, intonation, balance, dynamics, articulation, phrasing. All of these characteristics may enter into your assessment of the choir's, or a single section's, pitch.

WHAT DO YOU TUNE FIRST WHEN TRYING TO FIX INTONATION ISSUES?

Tune principal cadences to the overtone series by sensitizing the singers' ears to perfect octaves, fifths, and thirds. Listen to the overtones created by a fundamental low note struck strongly on the piano: octaves, fifths, and thirds are heard, some softer, some louder, but they are all there. An octave overtone in the air is at a 2-to-1 proportion. The fifth overtone in the air is at a 3-to-2 proportion and sounds ever so slightly above (sharp to) the fifth on the piano related to the fundamental. The third (5-to-4 proportion) in the air sounds noticeably lower (flat to) the third on the piano. Tune to these overtones at all principal cadences.

ARE CERTAIN INTERVALS WORSE TO TUNE THAN OTHERS?

Ascending and descending half steps and whole steps are the biggest sources for flatting. They are the impurities of the overtone series—the "Pythagorean[5] flaw" that shows up in half and whole steps. This flaw in acoustics is absolutely inherent and can be measured by comparing a series of perfect fifths. For example, using C as the fundamental, tune each successive fifth at a 3-to-2 proportion—C G D A E. The high E is extremely sharp and excruciatingly out of tune with the E overtone produced by the original C. The half steps on the piano, of course, are tempered so that every half step—in fact, every interval—is slightly out of tune with the natural law in the overtone series. This "slight" out-of-tune state shows up in all melodic formulas we sing.

---

5 *Pythagorean Tuning* uses the 3:2 frequency ratio for all interval relationships. This interval is considered to be the most consonant of all intervals.

Thus, we must sing ascending half and whole steps slightly wide to the tempered ones, and sing descending half steps and whole steps narrow to the tempered piano ones. There are twenty-two melodic formulas that always flat. They consist of every combination of half steps, whole steps, and minor thirds. For example, in the familiar tune *Three Blind Mice*, "Blind" is always flat, which means that "Mice" will be flat as a result. Interval leaps of a fourth, fifth, sixth, and seventh all create poor ear-voice coordination and inevitable pitch problems if not corrected early on in the learning process. The descending major third (the sound of *"door-bell"*) also consistently flats.

WHEN IS IT TOO SOON TO WORK ON PITCH ACCURACY?

Choral singers learn faulty pitch habits at the initial sight-reading/note-learning stage. Immediately correct pitch, as well as wrong notes, during those early stages. It is during this time that "associative pitch problems" develop—those problems that inevitably occur when new pieces are rehearsed and when "finding the notes in one's voice" create subtle difficulty in the initial ear/voice coordination—a natural phenomenon. But once the note is learned, one must not allow the "associative pitch problems" to be sung over and over with the same note and/or melodic pattern involving the note.

In essence, sight-reading produces faulty ear-voice coordination where singers too often do not land on the note squarely. Singers invariably and unconsciously perpetuate these habits long after the notes are learned. Good sight-readers may sing accurate notes, but the ability to sight-sing the notes well is not synonymous with the ability to "pitch-sing" the notes well.

WHAT CAN I DO TO IMPROVE CHORAL INTONATION?

1a. Initially, sing a composition (or part of a longer piece) and encourage the choir to create desired expressions (dynamics, phrasing, articulation, linear direction, rubato) as they learn the notes. This will create a context into which the note-learning process will have more meaning.

1b. Soon, separate text from the notes. Text consonants take time and influence good rhythm. Most importantly, singing on a neutral vowel, such as *oo* or a closed *oh*, is very helpful in creating a unified vowel that will inevitably help create unified pitch.

1c. Sing each note with a long *staccato*, or what I call "*legato doo* with space between the notes." Sing each note just long enough to develop good ear-voice coordination. For example, if a quarter note is at the tempo of 60 beats per minute, sing the quarter note like a sixteenth note and let go. Singers hear all the vocal parts moving, and not only their pitch will improve, but the ensemble rhythm will improve.

1d. In this way, a steady pulse will be perceived, and singers' physiological responses will be sensitized to the tempo the conductor wants. Once good pitch and ensemble rhythm are established, have the choir sing their lines on *legato doo*. The effect is often very beautiful.

1e. Once this sequence is confirmed, all the expressive elements can then be superimposed over a context of excellent ensemble rhythm and pitch.

1f. When the choir is really singing the composition in tune, with good ensemble rhythm and with the desired expressive elements, bring back the text. Inevitably, there will be an adjustment, and this will especially affect ensemble tempo. At this stage, I often have one or two sections sing with text, and the other sections sing *staccato doo*. This clarifies the real pulse and over time, ensemble rhythm, with text, will be re-established. In the process, unify the vowels within each section and between each section, especially at cadences.

2. Energize singers through exercise, posture, enthusiasm, humor, exuberance, love of music, and positive reinforcement. Stop rehearsing one piece if it keeps going out of tune and go to another. Try not to rehearse two slow pieces in a row. Try to work on different musical components over the course of a rehearsal—rhythm, dynamics, vowels, line, intonation, rubato—and contrast homophonic pieces with polyphonic pieces, loud with soft, fast with slow.

3. On long-held notes, ask singers to crescendo and sharp (very subtly, but with energy) to maintain good pitch. During warm-ups, practice sharping a half step over (say) 16 beats at 60 beats per minute. Then, practice flatting one half step over the same (this will be easy!) 60 beats per minute. Singers will see how difficult it will be to sharp "against gravity" and how easy it is to be pulled down by gravity. They will also learn just how wide a half step really is. The half step must be slightly sharp to the piano half step.

WE SIMPLY DON'T STAY IN TUNE! WHAT SHOULD I DO?

Once a composition is well learned, though not necessarily perfected, the whole may still go flat. If that is true, CHANGE THE KEY! Changing keys eliminates very quickly many of the original associative ear-voice coordination problems that have remained. Change the key up or down by a half step depending on the work's original key. This will change the physiological association of how the notes feel in the voice, and will counteract many of the associative pitch problems that have accrued over time. The piece feels fresh.

The new key will likely energize the vocal sound. An almost unconscious motivation to sing the right notes in a key that feels different in the voice and sounds different in the ear creates a new experience that automatically improves the choir's intonation.

ARE THERE TENDENCIES FOR CERTAIN KEYS TO GO FLAT OR SHARP?

Key characteristics (for unaccompanied pieces):

> F always flats
> C often flats
> G frequently flats
> B-flat normally flats
> E-flat frequently flats

I automatically change all pieces in F major to F-sharp major (and occasionally E major) and all pieces in C major to C-sharp major (and occasionally B major). Sometimes pieces in G major I will move to F-sharp. Pieces in B-flat I often move to B, though frequently to A. Choice of key depends upon the texture of the composition, as well as the preferred vocal color in which the choir simply sounds the best. Choice of key often, for me, relates to the text as well. The keys that seem to "keep pitch" the best are the sharp keys, especially A, B, C-sharp, E, and F-sharp.

IS IT APPROPRIATE TO CHANGE THE KEY OF THE PIECE BASED ON THE ABILITY OF MY SINGERS?

Refer to the chapter titled "The Adolescent Male Voice: Categorization to Maturation."

CAN I STUDY MY SCORE WITH INTONATION IN MIND? HOW DO I PREPARE MYSELF FOR TUNING ISSUES?

Know the score extremely well: harmony, melody, rhythm, and texture.

a. Mark and prepare to tune and balance all dissonances. Be alert to all dissonances that are difficult to hear because of the harmony itself or the denseness of the texture.

b. Circle harmonic and melodic intervals that tend to cause pitch problems.

c. Mark unisons and octaves, and look for fifths and major thirds in advance at cadences.

d. Circle melodic intervals that are difficult to sing, especially those that are wide or most troublesome, such as the augmented fourth and major seventh.

e. Circle chromatic changes.

f. Circle difficult-to-hear or unexpected harmonies.

g. Circle unisons and octaves.

h. In relatively atonal compositions or sections of compositions, search for "homing-pigeon chords": chords that, over time, will stick in the memories of singers and will reinforce their security at these points. Build a framework around, and a context between, these "homing-pigeon chords" upon which to place difficult passages. In time, singers in this way will develop readily found and aurally accessible points of reference from which to gain security in performance.

i. Write in reminders of sharps, flats, and naturals when singers (or you!) are apt to forget the key signature or when the singers may sing a wrong note that sounds "right."

Franz Biebl's setting of the *Ave Maria* is a staple in the men's choral repertoire. In the key of C major, this piece is hugely difficult to keep in tune. One must carefully decide whether to move this piece up by a half step to C-sharp or down by a half step to B major. Take into consideration the high A's in the Choir II first tenor line, but also the low F's for the basses in Choir I. Choose wisely knowing well your ensemble's voices!

CHAPTER 5
PARTS AND PLACEMENT

As a typical mixed choir sings in four-part harmony—soprano, alto, tenor, bass—so also does a typical all-male choir sing in four parts. The names of the parts may vary slightly or appear abbreviated, but, as they are in this book, are used interchangeably. Musical scores customarily list the voice parts in the following order:

VOICE PART NAME	COMMON VARIATIONS
Tenor One	First Tenor, T1, TI
Tenor Two	Second Tenor, T2, TII
Baritone	Bass I or Bass One, B1, BI
Bass	Bass II or Bass Two, B2, BII

Conductors, and to a somewhat lesser extent singers, must be aware of the clef used for each voice part. Melodies written in the bass clef require no transposition. Frequently, however, composers fail to use the *vocal tenor clef* (below) when writing for a tenor-bass ensemble.

Notice the number 8 at the bottom of the treble clef? This signals that notes appearing in this clef sound an octave lower than written, as compared to those in a treble clef with no 8 present. In this instance, the whole note on the third space is not C above middle C, but rather this note sounds middle C. It is standard practice for both tenor parts (first and second) to be written in vocal tenor clef, while both the baritone and bass parts are composed in the bass clef. It is also safe to assume that tenor parts written in treble clef—without the octave down symbol—are intended to sound an octave down from what is written. There are, however, examples of the first tenor line deliberately composed in the treble clef with an expectation of the voice sounding where written. Examples of this are seen both in early music and in some arranged or re-voiced works where the original scoring calls for a mixed choir.

WHAT ARE THE ACCEPTABLE WRITTEN RANGES FOR NON-MUSIC-MAJOR COLLEGE STUDENTS?

(Jameson Marvin) About fifteen years ago, I probably would have answered this question differently from how I do now. Oddly, as time has gone by, from my perspective (in auditioning freshmen for the Harvard Glee Club) male voices seem to be getting higher. It is very rare these days that we have a good, solid, low bass E that is not fuzzy and breathy. Many baritones seem to be more bari/tenors—not high and not low. First tenors with a high A still seem somewhat reasonable.

And so I would answer that question by saying:

Tenor One	low D, high A
Tenor Two	low B, high F-sharp
Baritone	low G, high E
Bass	low E, high E-flat

Generally, I find that singers with little vocal experience or those with modest high school experience find it difficult to reach higher notes. However, over the course of a few months, they become more comfortable in this register.

I find that basses who can barely touch a [high] D can sing a reasonable-sounding E-flat after just one semester. Baritones who can barely touch a high F can reach F-sharp by the second semester. Often tenors who sing high A have very good head voices or excellent falsettos; some occasionally have full-voice high A, but those are still pretty rare. Naturally, the lower notes listed above for both the first and second tenors will depend upon the individual, but frequently both can go at least a whole step lower. Sometimes baritones can sing a good low F.

HOW DO I DETERMINE THE VOCAL RANGE AND PLACEMENT OF MY SINGERS?

(JP) I find that being consistent is best for the singer, for the ensemble, and certainly for me, as conductor. Use the same technique or exercise to determine voice part for every singer to ensure all findings are equitable. To illustrate my point, imagine that Carlos arrives for his audition at 8:00 a.m. You have him sing an ascending five-note scale moving up by a half step each time. Carlos is able to sing a solid high E-flat and his low G is secure. His low F is present but has little core and is unconvincing. You determine Carlos is a baritone.

Later that day, Andrew arrives for his placement audition. Andrew missed the first day of choir, but you agree to see him immediately following rehearsal. Having sung tenor for the past hour, a decision he made himself, Andrew is unable to sing a high D. His low C (C3) is weak and sounds "fried." Is Andrew a baritone? Are you hearing Andrew's authentic register?

You have heard two singers who improperly prepared for their placement auditions. For most, early-morning singing is difficult. Our bodies are not yet warmed up and our voices are not functioning to their potential.

Refer to the chapter titled "Anatomy of the Male Voice" for rationale and information on early-morning singing and related topics.

High notes are nearly impossible to sing in the early hours of the morning. Low notes are fun and come easily. Conversely, Andrew may very well have sung in his falsetto for the entire rehearsal, leaving his entire vocal mechanism positioned in such a way that low notes are nearly impossible without first "warming down." Also it is likely that Andrew can't sing a high D because he spent the past hour forcing his upper range and is now so fatigued that his instrument refuses to produce. In both scenarios, neither singer is being adjudicated accurately.

There are endless methods for determining one's range. While every conductor has his or her own preferred techniques, let me share one that has served me well over the years. As I remember it, I picked up this exercise, or something similar to it, from James Litton, then director of the American Boychoir. Remember, the goal is to be as consistent as possible. I use a simple descending five-note scale on *naw* beginning in D major (first note sung is A). I tell the singer to rhyme the vowel with the word "dog."

Here is what I am assessing as the complete exercise ascends by half step:

1. Range. Is the singer able to sing the first note of the scale pattern? At what point does the singer forfeit? At what point does he switch into falsetto? How does that falsetto sound? Does he use mixture? Once in falsetto, does he carry that down or flip back into modal (chest) voice?

2. Is each onset of sound precisely in tune?

3. Is the descending scale sung in tune? Does the singer flat on the way down or keep pitch?

4. What is the timbre of the voice as it ascends? Is it brash? Strident? Brighter than in the lower register?

5. What note is sung most beautifully?

Most often, it is not the absolute highest note sung that I catalog as the top of the singer's range. Rather, I am interested in the most beautiful note offered at the outer edges of the range. This is where consistency by the conductor is vital!

In evaluating the lower register, I listen for the aforementioned items, but also for the following:

1. Obvious *passaggio* changes. The most obvious flip falls between the modal voice (chest) and falsetto (head) voice; however, in the lower register for men, there is almost always a change in action around D3 and another around B2 depending on the singer.

2. The second *passaggio* change listed above affects the lowest part of one's voice. It is here most often that male singers experience "vocal fry" or a gravelly sound.

Again, it is the most beautiful sound with which I am concerned. Be consistent and honest with your decisions. It's always impressive to hear a bass reach a low C, but in reality, his most stunning note may be the F above. It has core and resonance and is consistent day after day. This is the note I record.

Lastly, explain to your singers what you're listening for and how you're listening for it! Vocalize them to the extreme and let them know when they've reached the low C. Men love to show off just how low they think they can sing, but do tell them why you are recording the F and not the C. I keep yearly records in order to show singers their growth. Young singers find it especially interesting to see that from their freshmen year to their senior year, they substantially increased both ends of their range. Adult singers are also keen to know where they fell in prior years.

WHAT IS A COUNTERTENOR?

(JP) The countertenor voice has existed, in some form or another, since at least the Middle Ages. Defining and identifying the countertenor voice, though, remains a challenge for even the most accomplished voice teacher and professional singer. Two definitions have emerged as acceptable:

1. The countertenor sings using a developed falsetto in the alto or soprano vocal tessitura.

2. The countertenor sings with a light, unusually high tenor voice, which may also use some falsetto at the top of his vocal range.

By either definition, a countertenor has developed his falsetto enough that it has similar power and resonance of a male employing his modal voice. Often, the countertenor sound is compared to the female sound or that of the alto, mezzo-soprano or soprano and, while I believe the sound to be drastically different, the printed notes sung are definitely the same.

Refer to the chapter titled "The Product: Choral Tone" for further information on utilizing the falsetto voice.

DO MEN'S CHORUSES HAVE COUNTERTENORS IN THEM?

(JP) For all intents and purpose, the answer is no. Postpubescent TTBB choirs do not call for countertenors. However, both the renowned twelve-man professional ensemble Chanticleer, based in San Francisco, and the six-man British ensemble The King's Singers employ countertenors. In these two instances, both choirs sing nearly all SATB repertoire. A third professional choir, Cantus, from Minnesota, sings only TTBB literature and therefore does not have a dedicated falsettist.

WHAT SEATING CONFIGURATION DO YOU MOST PREFER?
DOES IT CHANGE BETWEEN REHEARSAL AND PERFORMANCE?
WHEN AND HOW MIGHT I USE A MIXED FORMATION?

(James Rodde) To begin the academic year and when music is new, I place tenors on the left and basses on the right. If limited on B2s and T1s, which is often the case, these two sections are seated toward the front and center.

When most pitches are in hand, I scramble all the tenors on the left and all basses on the right. I move them into quartets as soon as I feel singers are confident with their own parts. Quartet seating, to my ear, provides a more unified ensemble sound, better balance, and better intonation. Once in quartets, singers seldom want to go back to sections.

The exact spot for a singer in the choir's formation is determined by various factors that include the individual's vocal caliber and timbre, ear for intonation, performing experience, and sight-reading and tonal memory skills, as well as height. As a general rule, advanced singers are widely mixed throughout the ensemble.

(Ethan Sperry) It depends on the level of the choir. A typical male chorus usually does not have many practiced sight-singers, so I tend to start the rehearsal process with everyone seated by vocal part. I draw up a seating chart interspersing strong readers throughout the group. I place weak readers directly next to strong readers.

However, I do believe almost all choirs sing better when they are in a mixed formation. This formation helps singers hear, tune to, and balance with the other vocal parts and builds individual musicianship. In smaller choirs, this is less of an issue because the various sections are nearer to one another. As a result, they hear each other better. My goal is to have the ensemble stand in a mixed formation for the performance.

Two to three weeks before the performance, I create the mixed-formation seating chart. Louder singers need to be toward the center so they don't stick out. If the group is very solid on the notes, I may mix the singers completely with no one standing next to another person singing the same part. However, if I have singers that are still tentative, I often create a chart whereby two to three singers of the same voice part are grouped together—again with the tentative musicians being partnered with stronger ones. This concept works well for groups of all levels; even my ninety-voice, nonauditioned high school male chorus sings performances successfully when mixed in groups of three.

(Jameson Marvin) I always use a mixed formation in rehearsals and in performance. My goal is to create clarity of pitch, vowel, and balance. Sitting in TTBB sections inhibits these qualities. We sing T1-B1-T2-B2 quartets in each row. When we run out of a voice part, typically T1 to begin, we form trios then duets. In performance, when the group is standing onstage, I take care not to have a vertical alignment of the same voice part.

T1 B1 T2 B2 T1 B1 T2 B2 T1 B1 T2 B2 T1 B1 T2 B2
B1 T2 B2 B1 B2 B1 B2   T1 B1 T2 B2 T1 B1 T2
B2 B1 T2 B2 B1 T1   T2 B2 T2 B2 T1 B1
T1 B1 T2 B2   T1 B1 T2 B2

Teaching students to hear one's own voice part, alone, not influenced by someone else of the same voice part, breeds self-confidence, team effort, and great security. At first, it may be scary, so often during the first week of rehearsals the Glee Club sits in sections ("newbies" next to "oldies"); sometimes, after the first week, we sing in octets TT BB TT BB (again with oldies and newbies sitting next to each other). Always by the beginning of the second week we are in quartets.

Sitting in quartets allows for excellent intonation, matching vowels more quickly, and excellent balance within and between sections. Some say singing polyphonic or contrapuntal textures in mixed positions makes it difficult to hear the independent lines. In my experience, it only makes it difficult to hear where the individual polyphonic/contrapuntal lines are coming from.

The counterpoint in my performances of Bach's *B Minor Mass* or *St. Matthew Passion* is completely clear, as it was for all the Renaissance polyphony that I have done with the Harvard Glee Club: *Lamentations of Jeremiah,* Josquin and Ockeghem masses and motets, Palestrina and Victoria motets, etc. The lines are absolutely clear IF they are balanced and IF the vowels are matched—and MOST important, if we are singing in tune. Singing in tune, in balance, together, with matched vowels, forms the great advantages of singing in quartets. The pride, enthusiasm, and incredibly enriching experience—educational, musical, and inspirational—felt by the singers rehearsing and performing in quartets are absolutely unequaled in my experience.

"Rules are not necessarily sacred, principles are."
—FRANKLIN D. ROOSEVELT

There are practical norms and expectations that we, as choral conductors, adhere to when assessing the vocal timbre and range of each chorister. It is by gathering this information that we appoint singers to specific voice parts and sections. Assigning singers is most often done using a prescribed methodology of one's individualized standard of sound.

As in life, though, there are exceptions to every rule, and extenuating circumstances must always be considered when determining what is best for the singer and the chorus. Maintaining positive morale and a safe learning environment in our rehearsal space is important, and as teachers we must never forget to ensure the vocal and emotional well-being of our male singers. As conductors and musicians concerned with performance practice, it is our duty to put the art form first. Remember, vocal placement is not about tradition or camaraderie; it's about musical excellence.

CHAPTER 6
THE ADOLESCENT MALE VOICE:
CATEGORIZATION TO MATURATION

The word "adolescence" originates from the Latin word *adolescere*, meaning "to grow up, mature, or augment." Adolescence is most commonly associated with the various stages of both physical and psychological development occurring between puberty and adulthood. Physical growth, separate from puberty itself, and cognitive development extend well into young adulthood—presumably one's early twenties. Classifying the "adolescent years" requires more than just an association with chronological age; it also requires a thorough evaluation based on psychology, biology, history, sociology, education, and anthropology. Within all these perspectives, adolescence is viewed as the transition period from childhood to adulthood.

Many associate the period of adolescence, or the transition from boyhood to adulthood, with outward physical changes of appearance, yet there is little evidence to support this claim alone. Biologically speaking, adolescence is marked by the onset of puberty, including changes to sex organs, height, weight, and muscle mass, as well as major changes to the brain's structure and organization. Naturally, these changes affect the voice too. Cognitively speaking, knowledge and skill increase with the ability to reason and think abstractly.

The first signs of a changing voice are often missed, but include an increase in waist and shoe size, though not height. With regard to the singing voice, the first audible change is a slight tightening around A4 (440 Hz); however, pitches above remain freely available. This stage in the change lasts six to nine months on average.

There is a point in a boy's changing voice that should be, and often is, obvious. It is during this time of development that one finds the most extreme examples of regular shifts in modal, falsetto, and whistle[6] voice quality. In this stage, the vocal timbre becomes thicker in quality and warmer in tone and has fewer harmonics above. Singing range decreases and is often inconsistent. This stage in the changing voice usually lasts twelve to fourteen months.

---

6   The whistle register (also called the flageolet or flute register) is the highest register of the human voice. It rests above the modal and falsetto registers.

Normal characteristics of male vocal maturation have been categorized and documented extensively by researchers and educators. Most signs are common to all boys, yet some happen in highly individualistic ways. To comprehend what is considered normal, it is necessary to know what basic physical mutations occur during puberty and physical maturation. These include:

- Testosterone is causing the vocal folds to lengthen from the preadolescent length of approximately 17 mm to an average of 29 mm in the adult male.

- Increased collagenous and elastic tissues are causing the vocal folds to thicken.

- Thyroid cartilage is lengthening and tilting, causing a "laryngeal prominence," more commonly referred to as the Adam's apple. Note: An adult male's thyroid cartilage is roughly three times that of an adult female.

- The thyroid, the cricoid (the ring around the trachea), and the arytenoid cartilage (the two pyramids forming part of the larynx) grow to be two to three times greater in weight.

- As part of the overall physical growth that occurs during adolescence, the pharynx, oral cavity, skull sinuses, and thoracic cavity all expand, allowing for greater resonance and projection.

Teaching successfully to the needs of adolescent male singers requires a thorough understanding of the vocal instrument and basic principles of phonation. As choral directors and voice teachers, we are obliged to provide instruction per the norms of the various vocal register divisions, though, as is the case in nearly all educational instances, we face a variety of learning styles complicated by an adolescent male physiology that is ever-changing in unique ways and at a unique pace. There are, however, a number of identifiable stages that most boys' voices pass through on the way to maturation.

Educational researchers have used different nomenclature to describe these stages, and information on this subject continues to evolve and advance, but in recent history two such researchers have developed platforms widely accepted.

COOPER'S CAMBIATA CONCEPT

Dr. Irvin Cooper, professor of music education at Florida State University from 1950 to 1970, devised and promulgated one of the most recognized and accepted educational approaches to the changing voice studied and utilized today. Cooper, who began his teaching career in Canada, documented that young men had an ability and desire to sing throughout the duration of their vocal mutation—the change—so long as the repertoire suited their unique voice register and quality. Cooper believed choral repertoire should fit the voice and not the other way around.

In his research, Cooper coined the term *cambiata*, coming from the Latin phrase *cambiata nota*, meaning "changing note." He then adapted it to *cambiata voce* or changing voice. Having worked with and classified more than 114,000 adolescent voices throughout his lifetime, Cooper developed guidelines for categorizing young singers whose voices were in the process of maturation. He believed adolescent girls should not be classified as sopranos and altos, but rather as equal, and he used "blue" and "green" to distinguish vocal quality and timbre.

Cooper also identified four categories, or stages, of the male changing voice:

1. **Male Soprano**—the unchanged voice. This sound is full, rich, and soprano-like. Males typically remain in this stage until they are 11 or 12. Most sing the soprano part in a multivoice part choir.

2. ***Cambiata***—the first phase of change. This sound is known for having a "woolly" quality. The voice is similar in sound to the unchanged voice, while lower tones become stronger.

3. **Baritone**—the second phase of change. This voice is difficult for males to control. Most boys experience cracking between registers and a loss in the mid-range. Sometimes, the extreme highs and lows sound, but the middle section of the voice does not. While some experience this blank spot in their range, others may have trouble accessing their falsetto.

4. **Bass**—rare to find at the middle-school age. For typical ranges of the changed male voice, refer to the chapter titled "Parts and Placement."

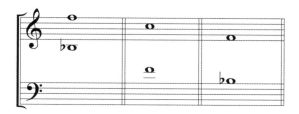

Vocal ranges according to Cooper

COOKSEY'S SIX STAGES OF VOICE MATURATION

Dr. John M. Cooksey first became interested in the male adolescent voice in the 1960s while a student of Cooper's at Florida State University. In Cooksey's effort to explain and synthesize elements of his own philosophies with those of other researchers, including Duncan Swanson and Fredrick McKenzie, Cooksey scripted his *Contemporary, Eclectic Theory*[7]. This theory consists of six separate voice stages and includes both high and low note singing ranges, as well as the notes making up the comfortable singing range (the tessitura). He recommends that boys develop and sing with a healthy tone and technique so long as they do so within the parameters of the stages of male adolescent voice maturation. According to Cooksey[8], they are:

I. Unchanged Voice

- **Speaking voice:** Light voice quality.
- **Singing voice:** Full, rich soprano-like quality. Typically, boys may sing too heavily in the lower range, therefore shifting quite noticeably when going to higher pitches.
- **Agility:** Very flexible with good capacity for dynamic variation.

II. Midvoice I

- **Speaking voice:** Light voice quality. Not unlike the Unchanged Voice, but the sound may be breathier.
- **Singing voice:** Loss of tonal clarity and richness in high pitches.
- **Agility:** Not as flexible due to increased size of vocal folds.

III. Midvoice II

- **Speaking voice**: Lower and noticeably huskier, thicker, and sometimes breathier than the Midvoice I.
- **Singing voice:** Huskier and thicker. Falsetto and whistle registers emerge. More stability in the lower range.
- **Agility:** Avoid the upper pitch area until the singer can learn to "melt" the transition area. Assign vocal parts skillfully.

---

7   Cooksey, John. *Development of a Contemporary, Eclectic Theory of the Training and Cultivation of the Junior High School Male Changing Voice.* The Choral Journal, Oct.-Dec., 1977.

8   Cooksey, John. *Working with the Adolescent Male Voice.* St. Louis: Concordia Publishing House, 1999.

IV. Midvoice IIA

- **Speaking voice**: Huskier and thicker than Midvoice II. Susceptible to hoarseness and abuse. Register breaks are very apparent.

- **Singing voice:** Extreme instability in the upper pitch range, where strain can occur. Tendency toward pushing. Transition to falsetto can be extremely difficult with some not able to sing in that register at all. Whistle register becomes more prominent. Singers have perceptual difficulties in matching pitch.

- **Agility:** Voice is weaker and less flexible. Be cautious in the use of falsetto.

V. New Baritone

- **Speaking voice:** Lower pitches are evident. Quality is thin compared to adult quality, but more consistently alike across individuals.

- **Singing voice:** Firm and clear, yet immature and lacking in adult quality sounds. Very little vibrato. The falsetto may "pop" in, leaving a "blank spot" in the phonation. Vocalises to lighten the upper range may enable a return of the missing pitches.

- **Agility:** Lacks agility and often becomes heavy when loud dynamics are called for. Frequent flatting occurs when overworked. Cultivation of a lighter mechanism and efficient breath energy in singing will enable increased agility.

VI. Settling Baritone

- **Speaking voice:** Thicker, heavier voice quality. Generally, there is more consistency in the voice production.

- **Singing voice:** More clear and focused, but still lacking in adult quality. Falsetto is clear and focused. Register transition area is slightly lower than New Baritone.

- **Agility:** More flexibility in upper range and in the transition to the falsetto register. Many boys still have a tendency to push.

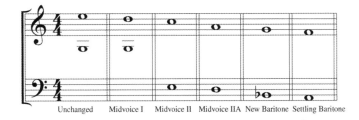

Vocal ranges according to Cooksey

WHAT METHOD DO YOU USE TO CATEGORIZE THE VOICES OF YOUR MIDDLE SCHOOL BOYS?

(Kari Gilbertson) I rely on the John Cooksey method for determining vocal range and I teach that system, language, and process to the boys choir. Because they are familiar with that vocabulary, I use the terms Midvoice I, Midvoice II, Midvoice IIA, and New Baritone when we are "collecting the scientific data" regarding vocal range. As a scientist does, we chart a boy's voice data three times a year, and throughout the year when needed.

After each boy's vocal range has been charted, we place him in the Bass, Tenor II, or Tenor I section. Middle school boys, in my experience, do not want to be called "unchanged" and have demonstrated disdain for being called soprano and alto along with their female counterparts in late elementary. Junior high school is the most disparate time for adolescents and especially for boys! Because the onset of puberty is so different during this time, I am very careful to make vocal range as matter-of-fact and scientific/clinical as possible. We emphasize that each will have a voice change in his own time, but no one has the voice of an elementary boy. Middle school directors should take care to impart a tradition where every boy's range is valued and appreciated.

A traditional boys school choir or children's choir has more latitude and expectation of its boys in traditional terms of soprano and alto, but the public school expectation is to refer to our young men in the lowered voice terms.

WHAT TECHNIQUES DO YOU USE TO FIND A BOY'S SINGING RANGE?

(Alan McClung) When early adolescent males are forced to sing out of range, the outcomes are frustration and failure. To encourage successful results, a thirty-second, individualized voice check can help the teacher determine the positive attributes of each voice. The melodic example that follows is limited to an interval of a perfect fourth and uses a skip rhythm and a set of innocuous words that are inconsequential. The goal is not to determine vocal beauty, but rather to determine the singer's vocal range and pitch-matching abilities. During the voice check, to reduce stress and any perception of judgment, the teacher should make lots of eye contact with the student and provide genuine positive energy.

Early adolescent male vocal range placement prodedure

THE VOICE CHECK

As the boy walks to the piano, greet him with casual conversation; ask him to say "hello." The timbre of his speaking voice should suggest his comfortable vocal range: high, middle, or low. Identifying the appropriate key to begin the voice check comes with experience. The more boys you hear, the faster you are at selecting the appropriate starting key. The teacher must be able to play the melody in any key without looking at the keyboard; your eyes and nonjudgmental smile should be used to encourage the young singer.

- To determine the singing range of male trebles, begin the melodic example in D major (D4).

- To determine the singing range of *cambiata* I, begin the melodic example in A major (A3).

- To determine the singing range of *cambiata* II, begin the melodic example in F-sharp major (F#3).

- To determine the singing range of the baritone, begin the melodic example in C major (C3).

HINTS FOR FEMALE TEACHERS

- When auditioning young adolescent male trebles, the teacher models by singing the melodic example (starting pitch is D4) while doubling on piano at pitch. The student is asked to echo what he hears. The singing should be relaxed and tension-free for both the adult female and the male treble.

- When auditioning *cambiata* I voices, model by singing (starting pitch is A3) while doubling on the piano at pitch. Student is asked to echo what he hears. The singing should be relaxed and tension-free for both the adult female and the male treble.

- When auditioning *cambiata* II voices, model by singing (starting pitch is F#3) while doubling on the piano at pitch. A female teacher who prefers to sing in her soprano register should model the melodic example beginning on starting pitch F#4 while doubling on the piano in octaves (F#3 and F#2). Student is asked to echo what he hears (starting pitch is F#3). Encourage relaxed, tension-free singing.

- When auditioning baritone voices, model by singing (starting pitch is C4) while doubling on the piano in octaves (C2 and C3). Student is asked to echo starting on C3. Encourage relaxed, tension-free singing.

HINTS FOR MALE TEACHERS

- When auditioning early adolescent male treble voices, the teacher should model the melodic example in falsetto, as written, on D4. It is acceptable to model the example down the octave starting on D3 while doubling on piano in the treble range, but the response by male trebles to the octave displacement is inconsistent. Some treble singers adjust and respond more easily than others.

- When auditioning *cambiata* I voices, model by singing (starting pitch is A3) while doubling on the piano at pitch. Student is asked to echo what he hears.

- When auditioning *cambiata* II voices, model by singing (starting pitch is F#3) while doubling on the piano at pitch. Student is asked to echo what he hears.

- When auditioning baritone voices, model by singing (starting pitch is C3) while doubling on the piano at pitch. Student is asked to echo what he hears.

WHAT TERMS DO YOU USE TO LABEL THE VOICE CATEGORIZATIONS OF YOUR ADOLESCENT MALE SINGERS?

(Francisco Núñez) The terminology for adolescent males and young boys is similar to voice parts found in the adult chorus world. In the Young People's Chorus of New York City (YPC), our young unchanged boys are called "sopranos" or "trebles" and are divided by parts with numbers from 1 to 4 depending on the literature.

What's great is that young boys do not really mind being called sopranos or trebles, and I have found, in fact, they like it. In YPC, we bring all our boys together several times a year. The older boys, with completely changed voices, have an opportunity to meet and sing with the younger boys, whose voices have yet to change. At this first rehearsal, I have the tallest boy with the lowest voice introduce himself to the entire group. I remind the younger boys that he too was once a boy soprano and went through a voice change. As a result, the boy is now successful in his role singing baritone or bass. The younger singers then take pride being sopranos and are okay with their voices eventually changing. I often come across boys who don't want their voices to change. When it begins, many are upset they can no longer sing soprano, and to compensate, sing in their falsetto range for as long as they can.

One of the funny ways YPC transitions boys from soprano to another voice part is how we place our singers, in sections, in the rehearsal room. Imagine a rehearsal set up with first sopranos sitting to the left of the conductor and the lower voices to the right. The door to the rehearsal room is located to the right of the lower voices. As boys' voices change from high to low, they move from left to right into the next section, which brings them closer to the door. By the time they are treble 4 (or soprano 4), they know I will soon be escorting them to the door. When that day comes, I shake their hands and wish them farewell. It is a sad moment, and other choristers both shed tears and applaud their transition. The girls never have this moment, but do have a sense of relief they will not need to leave. The boys know that the next step beyond the door is as a member of our Amani chorus, the youngest division of our Young Men's Chorus. We named it Amani because it is the Swahili word for hope. And, we hope boys will continue to sing and love their new voices. *Adieu* and welcome.

Rehearsal Room Set Up By Section

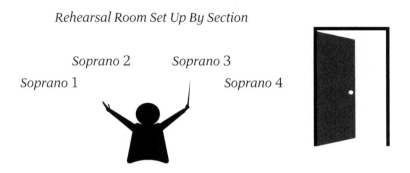

Why do you prefer the expression "evolving voice" to "changing voice"?

(Fernando Malvar-Ruiz) I make a conscious effort to use the term "evolving" rather than the more common "changing" when referring to *cambiata* voices. The main reason for this is to accommodate how the choristers perceive these labels. A big component of our work with young men is psychological. We must reassure our singers, build trust and self-confidence, and allay fears under circumstances that are often traumatic during adolescence. In this context, the difference between "changing" and "evolving" is subtle, but relevant nonetheless. Many boys fear their voice changing even though it is a completely natural process. The word "evolving" implies improvement and helps to assuage fears and uncertainty. Ultimately, both words are surely adequate and interchangeable so long as we do not refer to this process as a "voice break."

Some prefer to use the word *cambiata* to soprano or alto. What are the advantages of using the word *cambiata*?

(Alan McClung) The term *cambiata* offers the teacher and the student a label that promotes a special understanding and sensitivity for the unique timbre and range of the early adolescent male changing voice. The early adolescent male voice is not the unchanged voice of a child (soprano, alto) or the changed voice of an adult (soprano, alto, tenor, bass). The term *cambiata* also eliminates any unnecessary connotation associated with unchanged and changed voice classifications. Furthermore, it acknowledges the special pedagogical considerations of working with early adolescent males whose voices are changing, transitioning, mutating, and extending.[9]

WHAT ARE THE VARIOUS CHARACTERISTICS OF THE CAMBIATA VOICE?

(Alan McClung) The *cambiata*/phase A can be described both musically and socially. Musically, students experience the start of a husky quality in the lower tones and, at times, discomfort singing the higher tones. Socially, this early adolescent, middle school singer may have the pitches of the upper treble range, but simply does not want to be grouped with the sopranos or altos. He prefers a lower range classification to match his male classmates. Best practice is to oblige him. As the early adolescent male ages, the voice will naturally move down, not up.

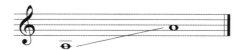

Cambiata I
Range of Phase A

The tone of the *cambiata*/phase B singer can be described as "husky, masculine and a bit chesty." For most of these singers, flipping into the head voice allows for easier access to the upper range, but social implications are often perceived to be socially undesirable by early adolescent males. Typically, when sixth-grade students sing together, males and females (age 12) are grouped into treble I and treble II. Male students in grades seven and eight (ages 13-14) typically fall into the ranges of the *cambiata* and baritone.

Cambiata I
Range of Phase B

---

9   Collins, Don L. *Teaching Choral Music.* Prentice Hall, 2nd edition, 2000. pp 146-150.

NOAH HAS A RANGE OF JUST FIVE NOTES. HELP!

(Laura Farnell) This issue is definitely what makes teaching the male changing voice a challenge! Not only do many singers have a limited range, but also one singer's five-note range is often a completely different five notes from that of another member of the chorus. Additionally, these ranges seem to change almost daily, so regular voice checks to determine the singer's range and vocal quality are essential.

I suggest a voice check at the beginning of the school year and after each major concert for a minimum total of four times per year. I will also gladly check a boy's voice upon request. Notating and tracking ranges is vital to the growth of your singers. I write the highest and lowest note performed by each singer next to his name on the seating chart. This is especially important to do at the beginning of the school year and serves as a basis for future voice checks.

When distributing new music, I instruct students to cross out words corresponding to notes out of their range. (Because many may not yet be proficient music readers, it's best they cross out the words rather than the notes.) It is important to choose appropriate repertoire for your ensemble. Be sure to select music that best parallels the vocal ranges of the majority of the choir. The goal is to have as many pitches sung as possible. I think discussing the scientific aspect of the voice change, such as showing a video of the vocal cords viewed through an endoscope, is very important. Adolescent boys should be taught that having a limited range or a voice that cracks is normal and does not make them a bad singer. Finally, be patient and encouraging with each boy—and with yourself! And remember the expression "This too shall pass."

WHAT INSTRUCTION DO YOU GIVE A SINGER WHO HAS LOST HIS HIGH NOTES? HOW CAN HE FIND THEM AGAIN?

(Rollo Dilworth) Let him know that it is normal for the vocal range to shrink during the voice change process and that the loss of high notes is often temporary. While it is possible that some boys may not regain their high notes after the voice has changed, many boys can maintain or regain some (if not all) of the high notes by continuing to vocalize in the high register during the vocal change stages. Starting on an A above middle C, have the boys sing descending *sol* to *do* exercises on a *loo* syllable, gently bringing the head voice into the mid-voice and chest registers.

Remember, while the voice is adjusting, a boy must learn how to use his new voice to properly access the new notes being added to the lower range, as well as how to access the old notes that were a part of the upper range. It is important to explain to young male singers how their voices are growing, developing, and adjusting.

MANY OF MY ADOLESCENT SINGERS "DRONE" AND OFTEN DROP OCTAVES. IS THIS NORMAL AND WHAT CAN I DO TO HELP THEM KEEP PITCH?

(Steven Albaugh) This sense of "drone" singing can be one of the most challenging issues for teaching younger male singers to sing at pitch and in tune. I don't like to use the word "normal" as it relates to the issue, but I have come to realize it happens for a variety of reasons. Let's face it—if guys are allowed and are able to drop the octave, they will.

By ninth grade, boys have yet to develop a sense for the physical aspect of singing. Ninth-grade men's chorus at my school meets at 7:30 each morning. It is the ideal time of day for young men to drop the octave! Adolescent boys are also the first to support the notion of "singing as an extension of speaking." It drives me crazy to hear "SUP?" and "HEY!" spoken in the lowest part of a boy's vocal register. Here are some techniques I use to help my singers match pitch more successfully.

1. How to use the spoken pitch to find a beginning singing pitch.

    Have the boy talk to you. You might ask him what sports he likes or what his extracurricular interests are. What pitch is he using to answer the questions? Begin your measurement from that pitch using a bright vowel. Challenge the boy to not put a ceiling or basement on his singing. Finding out a singer's range is as much a revelation to him as it may be to you, the teacher.

2. Find the *chiaro*.

    Chiaro means bright. A vast majority of ninth-grade males sing the way they speak—with a dull tone. It is therefore important that boys understand not only what the *chiaro* sounds like, but also how to produce it. I often use a bright *ee* vowel in my initial voice-building exercises. When a singer begins to feel he is reaching the upper extreme of his register, ask him to put his index finger at the upper midpoint of his forehead. Then instruct him to put the sound in his finger. This simple physical tool enables the boy to find and engage the resonance behind his frontal mask.

3. Choose repertoire carefully.

    There are times when no matter how hard we as teachers try, our boys will sing everything down the octave. When all else fails to work, I often assign bass solos to those boys. This isn't for performance, but rather for in-class experimentation and teaching. Sometimes I assign a simple folk song or college fight song to be performed in the boy's "normal" or "regular" register. Choose a song that allows the boy to sing the melody at whatever pitch is printed—high or low—but in tune. A momentary feeling of success will have lasting benefits!

WHEN WORKING WITH ADOLESCENT MALE SINGERS, WHAT IS YOUR CONCEPT OF CHORAL TONE?
WHAT KEY ELEMENTS DO YOU WANT TO HEAR?

(Fernando Malvar-Ruiz) When working with adolescent male singers, I strive for a relaxed, yet active on-the-breath vocal production, allowing for very flexible output. With the American Boychoir's extensive touring schedule, which includes a wide variety of venues and acoustical settings, as well as an eclectic repertoire, the ideal choral tone for us must first and foremost be flexible. It must work when we sing in a large cathedral with five seconds of reverberation, but it must also work in a theater with none. Our vocal production must be suitable to sing Tomás Luis de Victoria's unaccompanied repertoire, a work by Mahler with a symphonic orchestra, an Appalachian folk song, a spiritual, or a Colombian *joropo*.

I try to eliminate any kind of unnecessary strain while being conscious that singing is indeed a very physical activity. Many muscles are involved in producing a note, an interval, and a melody. The key, in my own teaching, is to train singers to use only those muscles necessary while minimizing or eliminating all other tension. For example, treble boys have a tendency to tense their neck muscles, jaw, and tongue, especially as melodies climb into the higher register. It is not uncommon to see a boy soprano's head face sideways when the upper limits of his tessitura are reached. At the same time, the rest of his body might be misaligned, ignoring those abdominal or intercostal muscles so important for proper diaphragmatic breathing.

Another key concept I try to instill in young singers, especially ones whose voices are still evolving, is quality over quantity. In most circumstances, given the choice, it is much better for the choir to sing with a beautiful tone than with one that is simply loud. Young males are able to produce quite loud sounds, and recess at the American Boychoir School is a great testimony to this! While we work under a general premise that no vocal sound is inherently wrong, we hope to instill in our choristers a sense of what is appropriate for any given circumstance, be it a particular piece of music, a performance space, or an activity. In each musical setting, our goal and the question posed is almost always, "How beautiful can we make this note and this phrase?"

Finally, adolescent boys whose voices are still evolving often sing with a breathy and sometimes husky quality. The breathiness is natural and caused by a mutational chink, and should not be discouraged. In fact, I recommend the opposite. I have learned, over the years, to love that tone, as it has a delicate, vulnerable quality so akin to their stage in life. It can also be a most useful addition to the color palette of a choir. Eventually, as the laryngeal muscles strengthen, this quality will disappear naturally. Huskiness, however, is the result of an overly throaty tone production. Working on head voice singing, with a relaxed neck and plenty of breath on the tone, should reduce this quality.

WHAT WARM-UPS HAVE YOU FOUND MOST USEFUL WITH YOUR ADOLESCENT MALE SINGERS AND WHAT DO THEY TARGET?

(Rollo Dilworth) I have found the following five warm-up exercises useful.

1.   Breathing with the Basketball

    Objective: To promote controlled, diaphragmatic breathing.

    Directions: While standing with good posture, pretend to bounce a basketball at waist level. While bouncing the imaginary ball, commence breathing pulsations in quarter note durations, making the sound "*tss*." When it is time to "shoot the ball," the singers should lift both arms to simulate the release of the ball and softly say the word "swish." On cue from the teacher, and without missing a beat, students can perform "*tss*" three times and a "swish," followed by "*tss*" four times and a "swish," etc., until reaching "*tss*" for the ninth time followed by a final "swish."

2.   Bungee Cord

    Objective: To access head voice.

    Directions: Place the index and middle fingers of one hand in the palm of the other hand (to look like a person's legs). The "person" should leap off of the bridge making a "siren" sound in high head voice. The vocal pitch should be sustained and change pitch according to the direction of the jumper. At some point, the bungee cord should snap the jumper back in an upward direction, back onto the platform (the palm of the other hand).

3.   The Minor Third Song

The Minor Third

Rollo Dilworth

4.   The Diction Song

The Diction Song

Rollo Dilworth

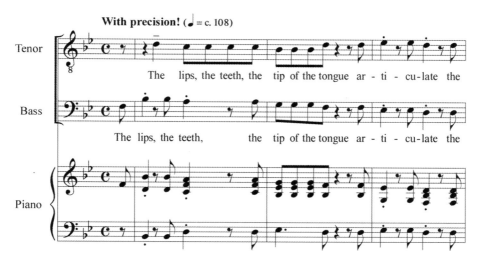

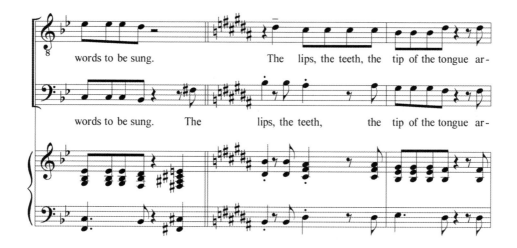

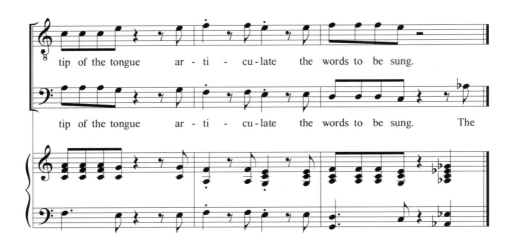

5. The Growing Phrase

The Growing Phrase

Rollo Dilworth

MY STUDENTS OFTEN GET EMBARRASSED WHEN THEY CRACK OR "MISFIRE" A NOTE. WHAT DO YOU SAY AND HOW CAN IT BECOME A TEACHABLE MOMENT?

(Francisco Núñez) Young boys going through a vocal change should be allowed to "crack." We can work very hard to find exercises and songs where no one cracks, but it is going to happen. If we prepare the chorus for when it happens, we can all laugh together. Therefore, before it does happen, we talk about it with the students. We tell them what to expect and assure them everyone goes through it.

When a voice cracks, which it will, ask questions of your singer such as these: What happened? How did it feel? How were you singing just before you cracked? Did you have enough breath? Was your posture strong? Was the note too high? Have the group discuss how we can all help to fix the problem. Offer ideas about breath, vocal tension, and registration. So often, a crack in the sound is due to lack of breath or preparation of breath, or not being able to maneuver between registrations. Have singers try an exercise to bring the head voice down to the chest voice, such as a light five-note descending pattern on *ng*. Allow a variety of singers to demonstrate this technique for their peers. It is so important to have a discussion about why we must sing through the change. Young boys should understand this is something natural and something that all young men experience.

Beyond the vocal misfire, I find the biggest challenge for adolescent male singers not to be the voice change itself, but rather the fear of losing the musical excellence to which they have become accustomed. When boys were sopranos, they perhaps sang with excellent children's choirs. The repertoire was of a higher caliber and they sang in important venues to cheering crowds. In a changing-voice chorus, young men sometimes revert to singing simpler songs with limited ranges and somewhat less public appreciation. In fact, many community children's choirs with young men do not have their boys sing as frequently. Some males go from rehearsing three and four days a week and singing more than ten concerts a year to just one or two rehearsals a week and only five concerts a year. This dramatic change has a psychological effect on young singers. Therefore, we must work to keep boys singing and excited as we teach and prepare them to move through the change.

THE PERIOD WHEN A VOICE CHANGES IS OFTEN A SCARY ONE FOR ADOLESCENT BOYS. WHAT CAN I DO TO ALLEVIATE THE FRUSTRATION AND FEAR THAT OFTEN ACCOMPANY THIS BIOLOGICAL TRANSFORMATION?

(Kari Gilbertson) In general, I use humor to diffuse tension or discomfort in my classroom with regard to both behavior *and* singing. There is no place where this is more necessary than in a middle school boys' choir! There is so much shame and discomfort around the changing voice with late elementary and middle school boys, and nowhere is this more evident than when a voice cracks. A voice crack is the hallmark of when a boy begins to doubt he can sing. Instead of a rite of passage, many see it as a time to stop singing.

I use several strategies with my singers that combat any negative feelings surrounding the voice change. One tool I find very helpful I learned from my colleague and friend Michael O'Hern. He says to boys, "Did you stop walking and running when you started getting taller? No? Then why would you stop singing when your voice starts changing? It is just a path to better options!" My own male students know that, like an athlete, a voice muscle goes through a period of change, but it is only a transition to greater range and success.

The phrase "voice crack" never fails to elicit a gravely hormonal, pubescent chuckle from my middle school boys. Therefore, we celebrate the growth that each voice crack foreshadows. Every singer in my chorus knows what part of his range is most vulnerable to cracking. As a reminder, there are posters on the wall in my rehearsal room saying, "Know your chasm!"

I also say a boy's voice is like a newborn foal trying to stand for the first time. Boys love to act this out too! The baby horse's legs are wobbly and he often falls down, but by standing again and again, working to strengthen those muscles, the foal is eventually able to stand on his own. I do not recommend re-enactments of "My Little Pony" with your adult men's choirs, but they work wonders with middle and junior high school boys.

WHAT SPECIAL METHODS DO YOU EMPLOY FOR TEACHING ADOLESCENT SINGERS TO SIGHT-READ?

Refer to the chapter titled "Sight-Singing."

IN WHAT WAYS DO YOU INCORPORATE GENERAL MUSICIANSHIP SKILLS—THAT IS, MUSIC LITERACY, THEORY, HISTORY, AND AESTHETICS—INTO YOUR ADOLESCENT MALE CHOIR REHEARSAL? DOES THIS ENGAGE YOUNG MEN DIFFERENTLY THAN IT DOES YOUNG WOMEN?

(Fernando Malvar-Ruiz) At the American Boychoir School, we try to incorporate general musicianship skills in each rehearsal. Singing in a choir, learning and mastering repertoire, and performing often should fundamentally be an enriching experience for every singer. Part of the enrichment comes naturally from the aesthetic elements of the music, but singing should also be fun. It can also be a spiritual time for many. Even receiving applause after a concert is enjoyable. However, as educators—"maestro" means, after all, teacher— it is our duty to ensure that this experience is also enriching in other ways. It is relatively simple to create a choir of "parrots" who repeat beautifully what we teach them without real knowledge or understanding.

With this in mind, at the American Boychoir School we work very hard to ensure that our choristers understand the music they sing. Among the topics we address are texts, context, social and historical circumstances, and the composer's musical and compositional choices and intent. We encourage critical thinking in the rehearsal and constantly ask for opinions. Of course, this works only if the choristers have a fundamental knowledge of music theory, history, etc. Such knowledge gives singers a full basket of tools and a vocabulary with which to develop and express a deeper understanding of the score. The result is not only a stronger connection to the music and its composer, as well as to the personal growth that comes with it, but also a much better performance.

Regarding the differences of appeal for young male and female singers, in my experience, young women are every bit as curious and inquisitive about the music-making process as young men.

HOW DO I BEST PICK QUALITY REPERTOIRE FOR MY ADOLESCENT ALL-MALE CHOIR? WHAT QUALITIES MAKE FOR THE IDEAL SONG SELECTION?

(Rollo Dilworth) First, I check for appropriate ranges. There was a time when TB (two-part) repertoire would work just fine. Given that a growing number of young boy's voices are beginning to change at an earlier age, I have begun using more TTB and TBB literature. Pieces that are scored for "high, middle, and low" voice parts offer more flexibility for boys with changing voices.

Second, I look for repertoire that includes optional pitches. By having optional higher and lower notes in the voice parts, the conductor (and the singer, when empowered to do so) can make choices about which notes feel most comfortable on a given day in rehearsal or performance.

Next, subject matter (text) must be appealing, engaging, relevant, and appropriate for adolescent male singers. The piece must also enable the singers to grow in vocal ability and general musicianship.

Finally, the repertoire I choose for adolescent male ensembles (and for all ensembles I conduct, for that matter) must represent a diversity of styles. Male singers should be immersed in lyrical ballads, folk songs, and popular styles. Repertoire for young men at this age should not be limited to sea shanties and "doo-wop" songs. Also, male singers need to perform repertoire that allows them to engage in movement. Especially during the stage of adolescence, boys need to channel their energies in positive ways. Music performance can be one of those healthy outlets!

What texts and subjects are appropriate for adolescent male singers? Sailor songs and sea shanties are terrific, but what else works?

(Laura Farnell) Upbeat, exciting sea shanties are definitely a great choice for adolescent male singers; however, I believe programming slower, lyrical pieces is also important even when boys may initially be reluctant. Composers often set emotionally sensitive texts to slower music, which allows boys to express through music those sentiments they may not otherwise be able to share or feel comfortably. Singing at a slower tempo and in a supported, *legato* style is also easier for the changing-voice male singer, as it allows him more time to think about pitches and facilitate intervals. Because boys consequently feel more successful performing these types of pieces, they often come to love singing the slower selections as much as, if not more than, the upbeat pieces.

What texts inspire you as a composer and what do you like to bring into your classroom?

(Laura Farnell) As a composer, I look for texts that speak to me personally, as well as texts with literary and historical beauty and value. In my experience, middle school boys balk at singing texts and pieces of music that seem "babyish." Instead, they much prefer music set to "manly" texts. I find that boys embrace complex poetry when the text's meaning and historical context have been explained.

Is it appropriate to change the key of the piece based on the ability of my singers?

(Francisco Núñez) The answer to this question depends on the concert setting. Is it a professional concert that is being critiqued, or is it an educational setting such as a workshop, family, or school concert? Also, who is the composer? Is this person alive or no longer living? If he or she is alive, call the composer and ask or suggest that he or she rewrite the work for your choir. If the composer is no longer alive, then it depends on the concert setting. If the concert setting is a professional event, then I believe it is not appropriate to change the key unless it is presented as a new arrangement. But if the concert is an educational or family event, then I find no problem with this. For example, most young instrumentalists grow up playing adaptations of larger works that have been made accessible or appropriate for their skill level. They concertize and are adjudicated on these pieces. Therefore, to change or adapt a choral work, as needed for singers, is acceptable.

I have created a flowchart to illustrate the options.

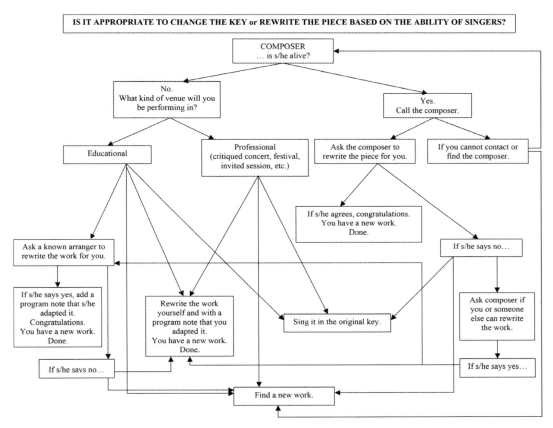

WHAT REPERTOIRE HAVE YOU PERFORMED AND DO YOU RECOMMEND FOR THE ADOLESCENT MALE CHOIR?

(JP) Refer to Appendix E.

Many ninth-grade boys stop singing after their freshman year. What causes this phenomenon and what strategies do you employ to keep them singing in choir?

(Steven Albaugh) I have seen ninth-grade boys in our choral program not continue to sing because of five main reasons:

1. They don't feel personally successful.
2. They don't feel choir is a manly activity.
3. They don't view choir as being as "cool" as sports.
4. They fear their skills won't allow them to join their friends in the upper level choirs.
5. They decide singing is not for them.

The question then arises: how do we promote success for young men in our middle school choir program? Developing a sense of teamwork becomes a priority. This can and should be done in every aspect of the choir experience, ranging from building musicianship skills in sight-reading to preparing and choosing concert literature. In my own school, I am grateful to have single-gender ninth-grade choirs. This makes it easier for me to encourage a sense of unity among the boys in my classroom. Our school's nickname is "The Irish," and we use this to develop the "Irish Way." We incorporate this constructive attitude into everything we do—how we treat each other as people to a certain style of jumping jacks in our voice-building exercises. This also has a positive impact on those who don't view singing as a manly or athletic activity. Upperclassmen who are actively involved in your choral program AND in school athletics have a profound impact on ninth-grade singers. Bring these upperclassmen into your rehearsal and have them talk to the freshman boys. Have them share their stories of how they approached choir from year to year. Your ninth-grade singers will feel encouraged and championed by those they admire outside the choir room.

While retention of singers is important, what strategies do you use to recruit new singers for your program?

Refer to the chapter titled "Recruiting."

CHAPTER 7
PROGRAMMING AND REPERTOIRE SELECTION

Programming is perhaps the most demanding task bestowed upon conductors, yet in many ways it is the most liberating job we have. I remember countless occasions when I sat on the floor surrounded by piles of music feeling totally lost. Do I create a themed concert? Do I focus on a genre or time period? Do I emphasize foreign language? Will my men's choir be able to sing this difficult, yet wonderful piece of music? Do I have the budget to buy this octavo for my entire ensemble? Will the school orchestra be available to accompany us? Will my guys love the piece as much as I do? Will my principal or dean allow me to use this text? The questions surrounding my choices mount as fast as the possibilities themselves!

HOW DO I FIND REPERTOIRE FOR MY TENOR-BASS ENSEMBLE?

(JP) First, it is important to let your music supplier know you conduct a men's choir. I also suggest you contact the large publishing houses and request the most recent promotional packet. Typically, publishers will send all their latest titles, along with some of their best sellers. The packets are often free and sometimes come with a demonstration audio recording. Search the Internet to find web addresses and contact information for the various publishers and then send a short email containing your name, institution, mailing address, and phone number. Inform them you are hoping to receive information on all available TTBB publications. Within a few weeks, you will have stacks of octavos in your possession.

Frequently, young conductors learn of repertoire and make their selections by listening to those ever-popular commercial recordings supplied by music publishers. Some may argue, but I do find these recordings helpful, as they provide a final product for you to hear. The larger publishing houses typically hire a small ensemble to record each work, so do not expect to hear a hundred-member choir. Vocal color and singing style, to my ear, lean quite heavily toward the pop genre and are not that of a school or community chorus. That said and with all bias aside, the listener is able to hear the entire chart often from beginning to end. Also, these recordings frequently feature a sampled orchestration typically available for purchase.

With regard to hearing complete performances of choral octavos, many publishers specializing in choral music offer online listening. Santa Barbara Music Publishing and Walton Music have wonderful websites that include such listening tools.

Growing your own music library does not happen overnight. For years, I have collected every program from every concert I have attended. I circle those pieces that interest me and order single copies for my library. When music arrives, I make notes at the top of the front page. For example, and using Franz Biebl's familiar setting of the *Ave Maria* text, I might write, "warhorse of the repertoire; lush, slow, needs good first tenor; must do." I keep my notes short so I can flip through titles quickly. On a less familiar piece of music, I might make note of where I first heard it or who recommended it; for example, "Jerry Blackstone, Intercollege Men's Chorus Conference 2009; tough rhythms; great closer." This system can save quite a bit of time when you are sitting on the floor surrounded by those piles and you are looking only for that perfect opener. Of course, keeping a pile labeled "Openers" works too, but one never knows when the perfect opener will also make the perfect closer!

Another place to find music is, of course, at the many conventions that are offered around the country. ACDA, IMC, GALA, NCCO, and Chorus America all have regularly scheduled conferences where publishers and music retailers display their merchandise. Reading sessions are also frequently presented. Refer to Appendix A for more information on these and other national and global organizations.

When browsing music bins at the various conventions, arrive early before others have the chance to rummage through the TTBB and TB materials. Often times, TTBB scores are buried among the plethora of SATB and SSA racks, so ask the proprietor for specific recommendations. Usually, the proprietors know the hottest titles and what's new on the shelf. Ask for honest recommendations.

Directors should also consult state music lists for vetted repertoire. Such lists contain available titles complete with publisher information, voicing, instrumentation (if any), and grade (usually 1-5; 5 being the most difficult). Texas, for example, uses a system called University Interscholastic League. UIL is responsible for local, regional, and statewide music contests for students at all levels; prescribes music standards; and maintains an exhaustive list of titles that have all been evaluated by professionals in the field. While UIL targets school ensembles, the resources are all online and available to anyone free of charge. Search the UIL Tenor-Bass ensemble repertoire list at *https://www.utexas.edu/uil/pml/browse.*

WHAT'S IMPORTANT TO KNOW WHEN CHOOSING REPERTOIRE FOR MY MEN'S CHOIR?

(JP) For all intents and purposes, this process should be no different from the one used for selecting SATB repertoire. That said, however, a review with a specific focus on TTBB literature is worthwhile.

THE TEXT

As a teacher/conductor of both secondary and collegiate choirs, as well as community choruses, I make every effort to stay up to date with what are considered "appropriate" and "fitting" topics for each of these age brackets. The two words that appear in quotes are certainly worthy of much scrutiny and thought. Rather than examine what may *not* work, let's examine a few texts and why they *do* work.

Robert Shaw and Alice Parker's unaccompanied TTBB setting of *Whup! Jamboree* (Lawson-Gould Publishing, LG51065) is suitable for high school boys. This Irish sea shanty is upbeat with "Heave-Ho" boldness. With regard to the text, the word "whup" is inherently funny, and high school boys love to bark it out during rehearsal...and long after. The imagery of sailing to Cape Clear, which lies southwest of County Cork in Ireland, and of seeing Holyhead and the lighthouse on Fastnet Rock provides great fantasy and intrigue. Furthermore, opportunities for cross-disciplinary education are obvious. This song is a good choice for both St. Patrick's Day celebrations and when students are studying European geography.

Now, my lads, be of good cheer,
For the Irish land will soon draw near,
In a few more days we'll sight Cape Clear,
O Jenny, get your oatcake done.
Whup! Jamboree.
O Jenny, get your oatcake done.

Now Cape Clear, it is in sight,
We'll be off Holyhead by tomorrow night,
And we'll shape our course for the Rock light,
O Jenny, get your oatcake done.

Whup! Jamboree, Whup!
Sailor, haul upon the line, Jamboree.
O Jenny, get your oatcake done.

Now my lads, we're 'round the Rock,
All Hammocks lashed and chests all locked,
We'll haul her into the Jamboree,
O you sometime sailor, haul upon the line,
Whup! Jamboree.
O Jenny, get your oatcake done.

Now, my lads, we're all in dock,
We'll be off to Dan Lowrie's on the spot,
And now we'll have a good roundabout,
O Jenny, get your oatcake done.
Whup! Jamboree.
O Jenny, get your oatcake done.

Socially conscious conductors freely change pronouns from "her" to "they" and "him" to "them," but it can be a challenge keeping the grammatical structure intact. Religious texts are also amenable to these adjustments. For example, there are many wonderful TTBB arrangements of the Negro spiritual *Didn't My Lord Deliver Daniel*. The last line of the refrain is "and why not every <u>man</u>?" In order to keep the text gender-neutral, some choose to sing "and why not every<u>one</u>?"

Perhaps one of the most popular songs performed by high school and university choirs is the famous chorus *Standing on the Corner* (arr. for TTBB and piano by William Stickles, Hal Leonard Corporation), from the 1956 Broadway musical by Frank Loesser, *Most Happy Fella*.

Standing on the corner
Watching all the girls go by.

Standing on the corner
Underneath a springtime sky.
Brother you can't go to jail
For what you're thinking
Or for the oooh! look in your eye

You're only standing on the corner
Watching all the girls,
Watching all the girls,
Watching all the girls go by.

Standing On The Corner
from THE MOST HAPPY FELLA
By Frank Loesser
© 1956 (Renewed) FRANK MUSIC CORP.
All Rights Reserved
Reprinted by Permission of Hal Leonard Corporation

These final lines are reason enough to give pause. Loesser's musical, especially this song, is considered a classic piece of American musical theater and very worthy of performance. While acknowledging the piece's historical relevance, consideration should be given to the makeup and character of the choir before selecting this work for performance.

Should a conductor choose overtly chauvinistic texts that are obviously flirtatious in nature? On the other hand, is it wise to be generic in one's programming and ignore significant genres and periods in our history? There are those who consider only the social and historical relevance of the text and how the work fits into society at the time it was composed, thus ignoring the ramifications of current-day attitudes. Such questions generate great controversy among conductors and educators of both SATB and TTBB choirs.

For high school boys, my own experience has taught me to keep texts friendly and accessible. "Friendly texts" are those about bravery, courage, strength, brotherhood, the outdoors, heroism, and even sports when you can find them.

Joseph Martin and J. Paul Williams' *Who are the Brave* (Belwin SV9216 ©1992) is a work with a text suitable for any TTB high school choir.

Who are the brave?
Those who go to war?
Who are the brave?
Those who fight no more?

Those who gave their lives

Protecting freedom's shore.

Who are the brave?

Those who serve in war.

Who are the brave?

Those who live with pain?

Who are the brave?

Those whose lives are plain?

Those with healthy bodies,

Those protecting the unsure.

Who are the brave?

Those who serve the poor.

Who are the brave?

Those whose speech is free?

Who are the brave?

Those loving liberty?

All those with heart and mind,

Protecting all they find.

Who are the brave?

Those who serve mankind.

These are the brave.

WHO ARE THE BRAVE?
Words by J. PAUL WILLIAMS
Music by JOSEPH M. MARTIN
© 1992 STUDIO 224
All Rights Assigned to and Controlled by ALFRED MUSIC
All Rights Reserved
Used By Permission of ALFRED MUSIC

The subject of war unfortunately continues its relevancy around the world. Loving liberty, honoring men and women who serve, and cherishing those who protect the powerless are all sentiments appropriate and necessary in our culture. These texts give way to earnest discussion on the history of war, but also the future of peace. Furthermore, and pedagogically speaking, there are many connections to be made between the physical strength associated with bravery and the physical support required for proper singing, such as feet planted strong, head aligned, chest not concave, etc. Making such correlations at every stage serves to increase every singer's learning and retention.

RANGE

Eric Whitacre's *The Seal Lullaby* (TTBB and piano, Shadow Water Music) is a hauntingly beautiful setting of one of the many poems found within Rudyard Kipling's famous novel *The Jungle Book*.

Oh! hush thee, my baby, the night is behind us,

And black are the waters that sparkled so green.

The moon, o'er the combers, looks downward to find us

At rest in the hollows that rustle between.

Where billow meets billow, then soft be thy pillow,

Ah, weary wee flipperling, curl at thy ease!

The storm shall not wake thee, nor shark overtake thee,

Asleep in the arms of the slow-swinging seas!

The text is suitable for any secondary or collegiate ensemble and the melodic lines are exquisite. Checking the extremes of vocal range—both on the high end and the low end—should be the next step in your review process. Don't fall into the trap of looking only for the highest notes! In this case, it is the basses who have not only a range issue, but also a tessitura one.

The Seal Lullaby
Music by Eric Whitacre
Words from "The White Seal" by Rudyard Kipling
© Copyright 2008 Chester Music Limited.
All Rights Reserved. International Copyright Secured.
Used by Permission of Chester Music Limited.

In this snippet, not only may the low E-flat prove difficult for many high school singers, but the line stays in the lowest part of the register for quite some time and may prove to be a challenge for many young male singers. Moreover and upon further inspection, this melodic line is crucial to the texture of the phrase. Whereas often a note can be omitted or a phrase sung up an octave, doing so here puts the basses above the baritones on certain beats, causing the melody to muddle the clarity of the intervallic relationships. This type of "quick fix" simply won't work in this example.

It is crucial to review both the highest and lowest notes of every piece before selecting it for your choir. Furthermore, one must evaluate the tessitura of each line to assure its appropriateness, too. Remember, a young first tenor can often sing a high G in full voice when approaching it by stepwise motion, yet a long phrase with sustained high G's may prove too much.

Dynamic indications for both high and low notes are also something to consider. For a mature adult male, singing a high A in full voice, regardless of voice part, requires preparation and significant breath support. That said, if it's marked *pianissimo,* most will sing this using falsetto voice, ensuring a beautiful, tension-free sound.

In Howard Helvey's *O Lux Beatissima* (unaccompanied TTBB, published by Hinshaw Music Inc.), notice the first tenor line. It hovers over E-flat for some time. The tempo is marked quarter note = 66, however this section is marked *meno mosso.* With that knowledge, a high school director may choose not to perform this piece for fear this particular section lingers too long in an area of the voice that is still developing. Age aside, E-flat is in the *passaggio* for most men (baritones and second tenors especially), making this phrase difficult to control at this dynamic. Directors of university and adult choirs should feel less trepidation, as the falsetto voice is more developed in those singers and the ability to flip between the modal and falsetto is naturally more refined.

O Lux Beatissima © 2009 by Hinshaw Music, Inc. Reprinted by permission.

Ensemble Size

Many conductors choose repertoire based on the number of singers in the ensemble. The rationale is that fewer singers make for a better interpretation of early music, while huge choruses are most appropriate for the romantic literature. On more than one occasion, I've heard conductors dismiss the notion of including a fine Renaissance motet in their program simply because their ensemble numbers are too large. Similarly, I know of conductors who would never program an opera chorus with a mere dozen singers. Not only do these decisions deprive singers of the opportunity to experience great music, but more often than not, the motivation for such decision-making is unsubstantiated or downright groundless.

What comes to mind when you think of Renaissance choral music? For me, the most noticeable attributes are a dense musical structure, lack of a clear melody, polyphonic texture, and the use of sacred text. With regard to sound, I often envision the performance venue itself—a church with a fabulously live acoustic, for example—and then determine the timbre I hope to achieve.

Ask yourself: What is the sonority of Renaissance choral music? Am I confident in my own ability to teach the desired period performance style? Is creating a performance in this style important to me? Is the edition I have useable and understandable? Is the concert venue conducive to this literature?

Questions such as these, of course, depend on the director's musical interpretation, but it is questions like these that should be answered when programming.

THE DECISION-MAKING PROCESS

Miserere mei, Deus,	Have mercy on me, O God,
Secundum magnam misericordiam tuam	according to your great loving kindness.
Amplius lava me ab iniquitate	Thoroughly wash me from my iniquity
mea, et a peccato meo munda me.	and cleanse me from my sin.
Tibi soli peccavi et malum	Against you only have I sinned, and done evil
coram te feci, ut justificeris in	in your sight, so that you are justified in your
sermonibus tuis, et vincas cum judicaris.	sentence and blameless in your judgment.
Ecce enim veritatem dilexisti:	Behold, you desire truth
incerta et occulta sapientiae	in the inward being, in my secret heart, wisdom
tuae manifestasti mihi.	you will make known to me.

Miserere mei, Deus by Gregorio Allegri is considered a staple in the choral repertoire and is arguably the most recorded example of late Renaissance sacred music. Countless editions are available both for mixed choirs and for single-gender ensembles. This is an example of a work that could easily be put aside for a variety of reasons; for example, the sacred text may not be appropriate, vocal lines are often problematic because of both range and length of phrase, and etc.

When reviewing various editions, tackle the obvious challenges first. Is the text appropriate for your ensemble? Does the text fit the concert theme if one has been created? Does the piece make sense for the season? A few quick scans can quickly and easily lessen the piles of music that surround you.

Using the *Miserere mei, Deus* as our example, begin by determining if this text is appropriate for the concert. In this instance, the text, while sacred, is from Psalm 51 and will not pose a problem for the audience or the singers or for me as the director.

Next, it is important to inspect the edition for the extremes at each end of the vocal range. Do this for every line. I often write each section's range at the top of the first page for quick reference. For example:

Section	Lowest Note	Highest Note
T1	F♯3	G4
T2	D3	E4
B1	D3	C4
B2	G2	B3

Are there other noticeable elements with regard to the notes themselves? In this case, there are two measures of simple *divisi* in the baritone line, as well as an opportunity for the basses to sing a D2 in the penultimate measure. Here, D3 is sustained above the D2, allowing for the lower octave to be omitted if need be.

Not accounting for the vocal spread of each voice part when making programming decisions can be disastrous for the teaching, learning, and performing process. Unfortunately, we have all been faced with rewriting parts when singers are unable to perform what is actually printed. It is sometimes easiest for the basses to sing up the octave when notes are too low, but in many cases doing this alters the texture of the piece, making it an undesirable approach. (Refer to the Whitacre example previously described.) It is also not wise to program a work for your high school men's ensemble that has the baritone line hovering on high E-flat. In this case, young baritones are still learning to use their vocal mixture and falsetto. As a result, chins reach for the sky, necks get tired, and improper singing technique is reinforced rather than encouraged. It is important to consider the singers' proficiency when choosing literature.

So far, the Allegri piece fits the criteria for my fall concert. The text is appropriate and I believe my singers can physically produce the notes at each extreme—highest and lowest. At this point, I might consider the length of the piece and the placement in the program. Of course, this will change and change again as I refine the repertoire list, but I might remind myself I already programmed four sacred works in Latin. Or, in this case, many editions of the *Miserere mei, Deus* are quite long. Do I want a nine-minute piece on this program? This piece might be omitted for that one reason alone, but it also might be included simply because of it!

Don't forget to review the required or suggested instrumentation for each selection. In this instance, the work is unaccompanied, but many works for men's choir require highly proficient keyboardists, a percussionist, or more. Some of the new literature now quite popular with college glee clubs requires instrumentation beyond the norm. Indian tabla, sitar, and taiko drums add much to any concert performance; however, finding these instruments and players who are skilled on them is often a challenge. It is also important to scan the piano or organ part. Do you have an accompanist able to play the keyboard part to Randall Thompson's *Last Words of David*, for example? Or two players for David Conte's *Canticle*? In this case, the Allegri is unaccompanied, but no one wants to begin the rehearsal period only to realize that the accompaniment part is more difficult than originally thought.

At this point in the decision-making process, it is perhaps time to hear the piece. Many publishing houses provide demonstration recordings free of charge, but one has to be very careful not to let this type of listening tool dictate musical interpretation. That must remain your own!

For those with some facility on the piano, playing the vocal lines apart or together, the full accompaniment, or any portion of the work will make a solid entry point to understanding the melodic line and musical structure of the piece. For those able to sight-sing vocal lines, it's wise to sing through each line as best you can and as close to performance tempo as possible. Be sure to evaluate how the line feels in your own voice. What musical and expressive qualities are present in each line that will suit your ensemble? For young choirs, determine if the vocal lines are singable and technically appropriate. It's important to look at intervallic relationships between parts, especially in the lower voices. Baritones and basses singing in close harmony below E3 (middle of the bass clef) often create a muddy and coreless sound. Skilled singers may face less difficulty in this situation, but care must be taken nonetheless.

In conclusion and with several editions in hand, the conductor decides to program James Rodde's edition of Allegri's *Miserere mei, Deus* (Alliance Music AMP 0611) for TTBB choir. Rodde provides the following notes on his edition:

All dynamic, tempo, and articulation marks are the suggestions of the arranger.

This TTBB version represents only a portion of the original nine-voice motet for mixed voices. I have taken the liberty of assigning the rhythmic values to the text in measures 27, 31-32, 40, and 46, all of which were originally notated with a double whole note. Conductors may feel free to generate their own interpretations of these syllabic values.

Rhythmic accuracy, a sustained quality of singing, and the expressive treatment of dissonances will be vital to an enriching performance.

WHAT ARE THE TOP THREE THINGS YOU LOOK FOR WHEN CHOOSING REPERTOIRE FOR YOUR MEN'S CHORUS?

(Robert Ward) As I look for repertoire, I am, at the most basic level, seeking pieces that are characterized by sincerity of purpose and integrity of craft. As artists and musicians, we have, hopefully, an intuitive sense or understanding of whether or not a work meets this basic requirement. That said, the top three things I look for when choosing repertoire are outlined below.

1. My entry point into a piece of choral music is text. Text is what fueled the creative impulse of the composer and text is the material that feeds my imagination and is what empowers me to inspire the singers. A great text can allow an average musical composition to live. Conversely, a fine musical setting will wither without a text rich in imagery and meaning. Text is also a key element in making a piece of choral music worthy of weeks of study and rehearsal.

    If choral music is to remain an integral part of the public school curriculum, then choral directors must select and perform poetry that is worthy of being studied in the classrooms of the English and literature departments. Text is a key element in making choral music competitive in a time-competitive arena (the public school day). Robert Shaw wrote, "music exists to convey that which cannot otherwise be conveyed" and "if everything could adequately be expressed in words alone then the arts of music, dance, and visual art would not need to exist." Using this as a guidepost, the texts we select for our choirs must withstand academic scrutiny and must be worthy to stand equally beside what is being offered in the dance and art studios. To do otherwise offers students a reason to seek intellectual stimulation in other places.

2. British music critic Henry Pleasants wrote in the *Agony of Modern Music*: "Music is essentially a song and a dance. And the farther it gets from either of those two roots the greater risk it has of collapsing and dying under its own weight." Of the six basic elements of music (melody, rhythm, harmony, form, texture, dynamics), melody and rhythm are the first two elements to which singers (and audiences) respond. Melody and rhythm are the initial points of entry and they serve to invite further investigation and listening. That said, I look for music that has a perceivable melodic component and a rhythmic structure or movement atop which a melody can ride.

    A perceivable melodic component does not necessarily mean the immediate ability to "whistle a happy tune," and rhythmic structure or movement does not necessarily initiate a foot-tapping response. Successful melodies are generally born of a composer who has an understanding of the voice. Is the melody singable by an average vocalist and does the melody draw out of the singer those vocal character-istics that are congruent with what is being taught in the private voice studio? Does the melody have a shape and contour that makes phrasing and dynamic shading ac-cessible? And finally, does the melody support the emotional nuance of the text? This does not, necessarily, have to mean overt word painting. But does the melody allow the singer to use the voice in a way that allows for an honest expression of the imagery and emotional import of the text?

    When considering rhythm, one must evaluate if the rhythmic and metric nota-tion match the natural flow of spoken word. Also, does the accompaniment provide momentum for the singers? This is especially important for younger choirs.

3. Does this piece match the educational objectives I have set forth for the choir? From the onset, it is imperative to commit to making the repertoire selection match the objectives rather than allowing the repertoire to dictate the objectives. Conductors must choose repertoire based on clearly stated objectives and must be ever cautious of falling victim to the folly of making objectives fit the repertoire. The former al-lows a conductor to chart a course of improvement for the ensemble—a course of improvement characterized by a carefully sequenced set of objectives that are con-tinually refined and reworked to match the mission, talent level, and development of the choir and its singers. Adjusting the objectives to match a piece of music is born of either a conductor who does not know (or is unwilling to search out) the repertoire or who selects repertoire for aggrandizement of self.

WHAT MUSICAL ELEMENTS DO YOU CONSIDER WHEN PROGRAMMING A CONCERT FOR YOUR UNIVERSITY MEN'S CHORUS?

(Jerry Blackstone) With a university level men's chorus, I often plan a full concert of approximately fifty minutes of music that is new to them, ten to twelve minutes of university songs along with twelve minutes of music performed by the resident a cappella group. A ninety-minute concert, from downbeat to "so long," is my goal. The ensemble I directed rehearsed 3.5 hours each week and numbered about one hundred singers.

Concerts are normally conceived of in sections, often with varying tempi, moods, keys, and vocal demands. The number of musical selections that make up each set varies, but my goal is to proceed from quick/*forte* through quiet and expressive, ending with the dramatic and energetic. This is, of course, a generalization, and concert groupings do not always coincide with this scheme. However, there is a strong desire to alternate quick and slow, *forte* and *piano*, and all points in between.

Sections are loosely unified by a musical element or programmatic concept. Examples of this include textual subject matter, dramatic intent or, in some cases, composer or genre of composer. Difficulty levels are seldom considered, but I am careful not to program a set solely of difficult or easy repertoire. The entire concert rarely centers on a single theme, as our audiences are large and quite varied in their musical and communicative expectations.

Concerts always begin with a traditional and recognizable piece and end with the university fight song and alma mater. Following the traditional opener, I always begin the "new" music with a strong, energetic, brilliant, and bold piece, allowing the men to fully sing and get rid of the vocal and emotional jitters.

WHAT, IN YOUR OPINION, IS FUNDAMENTAL IN CREATING A CONCERT SET FOR A MEN'S CHORUS?

(Ethan Sperry) This depends on how many weeks of rehearsal you have, but one rule I follow is that for each hour of rehearsal time you have prior to your concert, your choir can master (not learn, but master) one minute of music of the appropriate difficulty level. So, if your group rehearses two hours per week for six weeks, your group can master 12 minutes of music, which might mean two pieces that are easy for them and two pieces that will be harder for them.

If you are under pressure to perform a lot of music, consider repeating one piece from the year before or adding some "signature" pieces to your group's repertoire that they can sing every year. Signature pieces have the advantage of both bulking up your repertoire and building a musical identity for the group.

The Miami University Men's Glee Club, which I conducted from 2000 to 2010, ends all fall, spring, and tour concerts with a set of four pieces that are all big crowd-pleasers. We ended all our holiday concerts with Franz Biebl's *Ave Maria*. It was the responsibility of the chorus vice president to teach these songs to the new members, so very little rehearsal time was spent on them, leaving more time to focus on the new repertoire.

HOW MANY SONGS SHOULD I PROGRAM FOR MY UNIVERSITY GLEE CLUB?

(Gary Schwartzhoff) I often program concerts to contain four sets. I include four choral scores in sets I, II, and III. The fourth set contains both folk songs and university songs.

HOW LONG SHOULD THE CONCERT BE? OUR REHEARSALS ARE TWO HOURS LONG, BUT CAN THEY SUSTAIN THAT IN CONCERT MODE?

(Frank Bianchi) If the men are sharing the concert with another ensemble, I often program a set to be twenty-five to thirty minutes of music. If they are doing their own concert, I usually program for thirty to thirty-five minutes in the first half and twenty-five to thirty minutes in the second half with a fifteen-minute intermission. I allow for five minutes of talking/announcements as well. In all, a full concert lasts roughly eighty-five to ninety minutes.

HOW DO I CREATE FLOW IN MY CONCERT PROGRAMMING?

(Gary Schwartzhoff) In the first set, I usually feature choral scores considered to be masterworks from early historical periods. Set two often includes commissioned works for the ensemble and scores specifically dedicated to the ensemble. The third set follows intermission and features a small ensemble from within the choir. Set four features folk songs and songs of the university. I have not programmed concerts along the line of a central theme.

ARE YOU MORE CONCERNED WITH CONCERT FLOW OR MUSICAL VARIETY WHEN CHOOSING REPERTOIRE FOR YOUR MEN'S CHORUS?

(Ethan Sperry) I think flow is less important than variety. So much choral music is slow that audiences lose interest if we don't make sure to shake things up a little. I try to keep audiences (and my students) engaged by making sure pieces that are back to back have some kind of contrast, be that in tempo, key, use of soloists, use of instruments, etc. I find contrast of tempo to be the most crucial.

If you look at longer works by master composers—such as symphonies, oratorios, or operas—you will always find contrasting tempi from movement to movement. In fact, most symphonies have three faster movements and only one slow movement.

Some people just like to listen to their favorite slow pieces all in a row and are happy with a meditative kind of mood, but I find those people to be rare in most audiences. This is especially true if the audience is composed mostly of parents or friends of singers who may have little or no musical background. I think the goal of planning a set should be to keep the audience engaged, and that is done more effectively through contrast rather than flow.

Contrast can be created in almost any program, from a school variety show to a very focused program, such as "A Night of Brahms." I have witnessed "variety" concerts where the pieces look different on paper—a wide range of style, period, language, etc.—but the works all *sound* similar and thus the audience falls asleep. On the flip side, it is possible to do a concert entirely of works by Monteverdi and choose a combination of fast pieces, slow pieces, double-choir pieces, pieces with soloists, and pieces with instruments that are varied enough to keep the audience involved.

WHAT ATTRIBUTES DO YOU LOOK FOR IN AN OPENING NUMBER?

(Ethan Sperry) I prefer fast and loud opening numbers to ensure the audience is awake and paying attention. There are vocal benefits to this as well. We all know that creating a beautiful and intense soft sound takes much more energy than creating an energetic loud sound. Most singers, unless they are quite experienced, will sing a better soft sound after they have had a chance to sing loud. Also, fast and loud pieces tend to provoke a bigger audience response and singers feel great when they get a big reaction after their first piece.

I also consider vocal texture. Male voices singing in unison create a truly unique and beautiful sound, yet it doesn't have the same impact if the audience has already heard the same men sing in harmony. However, after hearing unison singing for a couple of minutes, the sound of a group breaking into harmony can be truly magical. I recommend that if you want to try a Gregorian chant or something else in unison, it is best done at the beginning of a set. This is usually the only time I might start a performance softly. This works particularly well for sacred and holiday concerts.

Many male choruses have a traditional opening number they use at all their concerts. These are usually fast, energetic pieces often related to school spirit that serve not only to get the voices going and energized, but also to build an identity for the ensemble. Many male choruses, including the Glee Club at the Roxbury Latin School where I used to teach, use Grieg's *Brothers, Sing On* in this way. It has an exciting musical energy for launching a concert and a text that all men hopefully appreciate.

(Frank Bianchi) For me, an opening number has to set the mood of the set or concert. My openers tend to be either up-tempo or a processional. I stay away from programming an opening number that is part of a two- or three-part collection of pieces or of a set of pieces.

WHAT ATTRIBUTES DO YOU LOOK FOR IN A CLOSING NUMBER?

(Ethan Sperry) I think the end of a concert needs more care than just choosing one show-stopper for the final piece; the closing number must be set up. One way to do this is to bring the audience down before you take them back up—in other words, I program my most beautiful (usually sad) piece in the penultimate spot and close with an uplifting, rousing number. The other way is to have two closing numbers—pieces that sustain energy and intensity, which audiences love, for a longer period of time.

You might also reverse the above and end the program with a showstopper followed by a very short, soft piece. This final selection acts like an encore, leaving the audience in a very special place emotionally. The famed British men's ensemble The King's Singers often ends concerts with a setting of *Simple Gifts*, while the Miami University Men's Glee Club ends most of its concerts by leaving the stage, encircling the audience, and singing *A Parting Blessing* (J. Jerome Williams; Shawnee Press). But just as I like to set up a loud piece with a soft one, I find that the soft ending doesn't work well unless a loud, showstopping piece has preceded it.

A real showstopper, to me, is a piece with tremendous energy, which is usually achieved through volume, intensity, high notes, and oftentimes rhythmic drive. It is not surprising that many choirs use spirituals or world music to close concerts, as so many other cultures' music has stronger rhythmic energy behind it than Western music does. Pieces with extra elements, like percussion, soloists, staging, or full choreography, also make for a strong ending.

DO YOU PROGRAM VARIOUS "GRADES" OF MUSIC FOR EACH SET OF SONGS? IN OTHER WORDS, ARE ALL YOUR PIECES THE SAME LEVEL OF DIFFICULTY?

(Ethan Sperry) It is crucial to have your choir working on pieces of varying difficulty. I like to begin the school year with one or two easy pieces that the choir can learn in the first rehearsal or two, so they immediately feel a sense of accomplishment and they have something to sing together outside of class. African pieces that can be taught by ear work well in this situation, as do fast spirituals with repeated sections along with many beauti-ful, slow folk song arrangements that involve a lot of unison singing.

I like to have at least one piece on each program that the group finds very challenging and maybe even out of reach. When singers learn a piece they initially thought was too hard for them, it brings a tremendous sense of accomplishment and pride. Singers may resist the piece at first, but the payoff is always worth it. Once they've experienced that payoff, they begin to look forward to the challenging pieces!

(Frank Bianchi) I always program various grades of music within a concert or set. There are some very impressive unison and two-part works available. I do not neglect those pieces when programming either at the high school or for the university men's choir.

How do I program four-part, quality literature when I don't have balanced numbers of singers among sections?

(Paul Rardin) I see two possible approaches to this and can imagine using them in combination:

1. Program music with fewer than four parts to avoid extreme ranges and difficult harmonies. Bach's two-part *Der Herr segne euch* from Cantata No. 196 (published in choral form for TB, arr. by Barry Talley, Hal Leonard Corporation) would allow half of your group to sing in their natural register and the other half to develop their up-per mixture/falsetto register. One might try rehearsing it such that each singer learns both parts and you decide on concert night which half will sing which part!

2. Encourage ten of your singers to "graduate" from one voice part to another. I have frequently invited baritones in my collegiate men's ensemble to sing tenor one for a semester to develop their upper register (both their mixture and their falsetto). Doing so adds real richness and warmth to the sound—even with those true baritones sing-ing in their falsetto. To fill out second tenor and bass parts, consider a rotation plan that assigns the same singer to different parts on different pieces. This avoids overly taxing any one singer by singing in a register that might be uncomfortable for him.

Please provide a sample of your concert programming.

Refer to Appendix D.

I HAVE TOO MANY BARITONES! WHAT DO I DO? HOW DO I PROGRAM?

(Robert Ward) The first things to remember are that you are not alone and that this situation is not unique to your choir. Your first step is to convince the baritones that falsetto is an expressive and usable part of the voice. Teach them to sing in falsetto and then build the lower range by coming out of the falsetto. No singer should be made to sing in falsetto all the time. Choose three-part literature and rotate the singers between parts. Each singer gets a designation (A-B-C). Tell the "A" group that on piece #1 they sing the baritone part. On piece #2 they sing the tenor part. And if it is pedagogically and vocally responsible, have them sing the bass part on piece #3. The premise here is that while they may all be baritones, they do not always have to sing the baritone line. Their voices are capable of much more.

Conductors must select repertoire that does not require a full-voice *forte* in order to achieve satisfactory musical results. Franz Schubert wrote music for male choirs, but much of it is not doable unless you have a tenor section that can sing a high G or A with full voice. Look for repertoire that can be sung well with much of the tenor line being sung in falsetto. Things to consider are dynamic requirements in the top range, whether or not the melodic construction allows the singers to move to the high notes via step-wise motion, and the tessitura (where the largest percentage of the notes sit in the voice).

Tonal balance is critical in this situation. Because the falsetto voice is lighter, and therefore softer in terms of dynamic, the balance must be predicated on the size of the tenor sound. Establish the maximum and minimum amount of sound the falsetto voices can create and then adjust the dynamics on the printed page accordingly. For example, a baritone singing A-natural (top line of the bass staff) can easily overpower a baritone singing a G-natural (second line treble staff) in falsetto. The section dynamic might best be adjusted by numbers—specifically, how many singers on each part. That number may change from piece to piece or even from measure to measure. Remember, not every singer has to sing the same line throughout the course of the composition. The conductor's ear must determine what is an appropriate balance.

Terminus by Nancy Hill Cobb is a perfect piece for an all-baritone choir. The unison opening is mid-range for all singers, and the constant motion in the piano part creates a rhythmic momentum that allows the singers to sing on the breath but with not a lot of vocal weight. The piece moves into two parts at measure 16 and then into three parts at measure 27. All voices could, or should, learn all parts so they experience singing in both full voice and falsetto. Once that is accomplished, the experienced ear of the conductor will determine how many (and which) singers should sing the top, middle, or bottom part. Balance of chord tones is important. The largest percentage of singers may need to be on the middle part so it is heard. As the piece comes to a close, the unison texture returns, recalling the *mezzo piano* dynamic and the buoyant vocal texture of the opening.

Terminus

Ralph Waldo Emerson

Nancy Hill Cobb

RECOGNIZING THAT EVERY CURRICULUM IS DIFFERENT, HOW MANY CONCERTS MIGHT I SCHEDULE OVER THE COURSE OF A SINGLE SCHOOL YEAR? WHAT TIME OF YEAR IS BEST?

(Christopher Aspaas) The male chorus is a unique animal. In order to determine what the right number of performances is and when they should occur, one has to decide what drives the need for performance. Are performances a part of a tradition, or are they something required? For example, St. Olaf College Viking Chorus, the all-men's chorus, is expected to sing two works for the annual Christmas Festival. The ensemble also participates in nine mass-choir selections, hymns, etc., on that same program. Some performances are in response to current events; for example, the dedication of a new building, a celebration of a community member, the response to a tragic event in the community. For most choruses, I imagine the requirements lie somewhere in the middle.

Men require *action*. One of the greatest "ensemble-killers" for male singers is a lack of opportunity to share the results of their investment. For the Viking Chorus, if we are not publicly sharing our work at least once a month in some fashion, our momentum slows and quickly deteriorates.

I believe a collaborative event of some kind early in the fall should be a requirement. Find a few pieces that will work—don't worry about starting work on that really hard piece you hope to present on your December program. With proper planning, you will be able to devote plenty of time to that challenging work later in the semester. One of our primary goals for the first month is to develop *esprit de corps* and a sense of ownership, for without these the ensemble will struggle for the whole year. At St. Olaf, our first concert of the year is at a shared event during Family Weekend. This concert is typically in the fourth week of classes. Two instrumental ensembles along with two choral ensembles prepare a brief set each, don formal attire, and share their music. This is one of the most exciting concerts of the season for my men because it is the first time they are in uniform and they look and feel like a real ensemble.

The next major performance typically occurs around the holidays, in early to mid-December. Again, a collaborative concert is great, as it allows you to delve into more challenging repertoire and not be solely responsible for an entire concert program.

Men require *variety*. I suggest finding ways for your ensemble to perform what many call "Random Acts of Art." Once a month, the Viking Chorus storms across campus singing throughout the administration building, the science building, the main library, the cafeteria, and the student center. We have even raided a women's soccer game *Braveheart*-style while singing the St. Olaf fight song (which is unfortunately a waltz in 3/4 time). These breaks in the normal sequence of the rehearsal cycle are key to maintaining energy and enthusiasm as pressures of the season build.

There is an amazing other benefit to this kind of activity as well; you begin to build a desire in places where there was previously no expectation of music. My colleagues in the sciences ask me at faculty meetings when to expect us next. I received this note from an administrative assistant who heard us one February. It read:

Thank you for coming to the administration building today! It is such a day-brightener to be entertained by you—especially on a cold wintery day. You sound TERRIFIC!!

These may not necessarily seem to be priorities that most guys care about, but my students remind me often just how important these experiences are for them as well.

Spring (April/May) is time for the largest program of the season. If one has carefully programmed since day one, an entire hour-long program can be derived from the repertoire assembled all year long. With home-stays and donated meals, touring with an ensemble does not have to be a budget-killer and will lead to the development of lifelong relationships and memories. Find out where your singers have connections and take advantage of local relationships. You are much more likely to have an inspired outing when your audience has ownership of one or more of the singers.

Men require *mission*. Why do men sing? Perhaps a better question is why *don't* men sing?

1. Acts of art by men that are not driven by popular culture are traditionally not supported.

2. It is easier to join an athletic team and, in many ways, is culturally expected.

3. As they struggled through the first adolescent vocal transition, they were not given the tools to be vocally or musically successful.

4. There isn't enough time.

Each and every ensemble needs a mission and a set of goals. The following goals were established for the Viking Chorus: brotherhood, integrity, musical excellence, respect, service, spirit, and vocal and musical development. If one lets the goals of the ensemble drive the need for performance, then the ensemble will thrive on the need to perform. For example, why tour? The answer is that touring builds brotherhood, provides the opportunity to practice and share musical excellence, and allows us to display proudly our school spirit.

Many of my colleagues here in Minnesota have used January as a time to gather their male choruses in a festival setting, since most ensembles can readily reuse repertoire from the fall. The sharing of music between community, college, and high school ensembles is a learning experience for all and one that we must do more of if we wish to thrive. While we may provide amazing experiences for our men, are we preparing them to seek out and celebrate a lifetime filled with music?

How many concerts each year? As many as we can!

When? As often as we can!

HOW DO YOU CONSTRUCT A SEASON FOR YOUR COMMUNITY MEN'S CHORUS?

(Diane Loomer) Typical choral seasons usually consist of three popular performance times: fall, Christmas, and spring. I prefer, however, to avoid the more popular concert times in favor of the following season:

A FALL CONCERT OF REMEMBRANCE

What turned out to be an ideal fall opportunity for a men's choir was a concert sung on November 11 (Remembrance Day in Canada). We commemorate this holiday with gatherings, often at cenotaphs, to honor those who died in wars. Chor Leoni's first Remembrance Day concert was titled "Songs of War and Peace," in which the choir sang a selection of songs associated with wars and the hope for peace. Veterans and their families, as well as those wanting to remember loved ones, were invited to attend. Our first performance sold out and the concert has continued to do so ever since. After twenty years, the theme has expanded to include world peace, remembering absent and departed loved ones, and extending compassion for all who suffer. In other words, it has become a sort of international Remembrance/Peace Day concert. This idea also gives me the opportunity to explore some marvelous repertoire from all around the world. It has now become a fixture in the local choral calendar, and we often have to present the concert three, sometimes four times to accommodate the number of patrons wanting a ticket. The formula is rather unique in that it has always been a concert of choral music with accompanying readings presented without applause. At its conclusion, the audience departs in silence.

TWO OPTIONS FOR A CHRISTMAS CONCERT

The original plan was never to offer a Christmas concert, as every choir in the city presents such an event. Eventually, however, Chor Leoni's audiences began to ask why we didn't give a Christmas concert, and thus we now offer two options:

1. Winter Solstice. This concert takes place on or about December 21 and has a musical emphasis focusing on the winter solstice and return of light to the earth. Although these concerts take a lot of planning and research, mainly to find enough repertoire and to devise creative staging, they have also been tremendously successful.

2. Warm and Fuzzy. This concert uses several familiar, more comfortable tunes and usually includes a sing-along. The concert is scheduled as near to Christmas Eve as possible and the emphasis is placed on calmness, serenity, and candlelit quietness.

A Cerebral Spring Concert

At this time of year we try to stretch the brains, ears, vocal technique, and tongues of our singers by programming difficult, erudite repertoire. Selections are chosen from the early music, romantic, and classical periods, as well as from the twentieth and twenty-first centuries. We also offer newly composed and commissioned works at this time. Since there is a longer time to prepare for this performance (from early January through March/April), it gives us the luxury of rehearsal time to get our teeth into the "meatier" repertoire. Originally, we didn't expect big audiences for this concert, yet it has become a hit with our more discerning audience members.

Summer Solstice Concert

The craziest of our ideas was to do a concert in June when other choirs had already begun their summer break. We call it our "Summer Solstice Serenade" and it is offered on or as near to the summer solstice, usually June 21, as we can. The concert is not one's typical choral concert where the choir stands in straight lines in a church or concert hall. Here in Vancouver, we learned of a summer Shakespeare festival held outdoors under a tent. We then persuaded the festival management to let us use the tent on its nights off. We first tried to sing fairly serious serenade repertoire, but the acoustics and the ambience opened up the possibilities of performing pop, folk, and show tunes, and allowed us to cavort in tails and top hats, canes, rain slickers, cowboy hats, and hockey jerseys. Remember, we are in Canada, after all! This light-hearted concert accomplishes two fantastic things for the choir: audiences have fun and become fans and regular patrons, and it attracts an audience of young people and talented young singers, many of whom are enthused enough to want to audition for the choir.

How do I select repertoire to bring on tour?

(JP) There are many options and approaches one can take when selecting tour repertoire. It is, of course, wise to bring repertoire that best displays your men's sound and choral aptitude. Because a tour is often the culmination of a year's worth of rehearsal preparation, it is sensible to begin programming your entire season's literature with the tour in mind. This is not to say every piece your men sing during the school year has to be performed on tour, but try adding a set of sacred (or sacred-like), non-Christmas music to your December concert. For example, begin with Randol Alan Bass' setting of the *Gloria* (Canticle Distributing RBM-101A) text followed by Kurt Bestor's *Prayer of the Children* (Alfred Publishing CH96165) and conclude with Theron Kirk's rousing *Promised Land*

(Oxford University Press 9780193860506). All three pieces would be considered appropriate for the holiday season and all three pieces would be solid choices for one's tour repertoire.

Many years ago, I remember attending a performance by the amazing Russian men's choir Chorovaya Akademia. The centerpiece that evening was Tchaikovsky's *Liturgy of St. John Chrysostom*. After intermission, the men returned to the stage no longer wearing their brown, monk-like robes, and offered thirty minutes of Russian folk songs, including the famous folk song *Kalinka* and other traditional dance settings. The audience was presented with a masterwork rarely heard—the Tchaikovsky—and was then entertained with this lighthearted literature.

What I remember most fondly of this performance and my reason for including this story here was Chorovaya's encore. The final selection that evening was the American Civil War song *When Johnny Comes Marching Home*. Hearing American music sung by a Russian choir is truly an unforgettable experience. Since that time, I have tried to include at least one number in every tour program representative of the country in which we are performing. Sometimes it is the national anthem and sometimes it's a popular song or familiar folk melody. The goal here is to provide the same memorable experience for our audience as Chorovaya Akademia did for me.

ANNOUNCEMENTS GIVEN FROM THE STAGE ARE AN INTEGRAL PART OF MOST PERFORMANCES. WHAT'S THE BEST WAY TO OFFER THESE AND WHEN?
(JP) For some, making announcements from the stage is a very natural thing to do. For others, however, if not fully prepared ahead of time, the announcements are brutal for both conductor and audience member alike. Some conductors rarely address an audience during the concert, yet some conductors do so between each and every selection. Whatever your preference, it is vital to remember the following before you turn on the microphone:

- Be prepared before you speak! Know what message you want to convey to your audience and have the words to do so adequately. One risks faltering and mumbling when the ideas are not well thought out.

- When you do speak, be informative and stay on topic. It's perfectly acceptable to talk about future concert dates or the merchandise available in the lobby for purchase, but be sure what you say is relevant and of interest to others.

- Avoid rambling and rambling and rambling and rambling and rambling and rambling.

- Be sure you can be heard. Use a microphone if available. Be proud, but not so proud to think that you are able to project to every corner of the room. If there is a microphone turned on, use it.

- Know your audience. True story: Several years ago, a university glee club came to a town nearby. A scheduling conflict prevented me from attending its formal evening concert, but I was invited to hear the group sing that morning at a local middle school. At the start of this mini-performance, the director graciously welcomed the sixth-, seventh-, and eighth-graders to the assembly. He then began to speak about the first musical selection, Pablo Casal's setting for men of the *O Vos Omnes* text (Tetra Music TC242). His monologue, which was also printed in a program and handed out to each student, went like this:

  > *O Vos Omnes is a church responsory from the Book of Lamentations. Jeremiah possibly composed it during the exile of the Hebrew people in the land of Assyria. The early church used such a passage to highlight Christ's sufferings as he approached the cross and was nailed to the cross. For centuries, it has been a flagship work during Holy Week devotions.*

  The performance was stellar and the audience was terrifically well-behaved. Moreover, the sampling of repertoire was expansive and covered early music through the most modern of choral writing. If only the director had been able to relate to his audience—eleven- and twelve-year-olds—this would have been a truly exceptional learning opportunity for everyone involved. Regardless, any exposure to fine men's choirs is important and worthwhile.

- Use your singers! As is said, "Variety is the spice of life." While audiences definitely want to hear the conductor speak, singers also make fine announcers. Some save this for the school spirit songs; when I was in the University of Michigan Men's Glee Club, it was a huge honor to announce the fight songs *Varsity* and *The Victors!* Encourage your singers to think out of the box when they are assigned to make the announcement. Perhaps they might set their comments to music. This is especially effective when promoting the most recent recording or fund-raising effort. There are many melodies to which one could set such an announcement that would make it much more memorable to the audience. "Please support the Titan Men's Chorus and get your car washed this weekend..." is truly uninspired, but sing it to the 1976 hit *Car Wash* by Rose Royce and not only will you get smiles, but the date will likely be remembered.

HOW DO STAGE ANNOUNCEMENTS ON TOUR DIFFER FROM THOSE MADE ON THE "HOME" STAGE?

In addition to including familiar music in the tour repertoire (refer to the chapter titled "Travel"), it is enormously effective to make concert announcements, or at least the opening remarks, in the language of that land. A note of personal preference: Audiences want to hear your choir sing first. I highly suggest that announcements follow the first song or set of songs. In 2010, the Turtle Creek Chorale traveled to Spain for ten days. After our opening number in Madrid, I read aloud the following:

Buenas Noches! Estamos entusiasmados de estar aquí en España y además saber que su equipo de futbol está en plena competición en el mundial de fútbol!

Este tour pone fin a la temporada que representa el 30 aniversario de la "Turtle Creek Chorale." En realidad, es la segunda vez que actuamos en España, la primera fué en 1995.

El repertorio que ustedes escucharán hoy representa los distintos estilos que normalmente nosotros interpretamos en Estados Unidos. Cada canción de nuestro programa tiene un significado especial para nosotros como conjunto vocal. Esperamos pues disfruten la música que nosotros hemos cuidado con mucho cariño.

Por favor les pido no se acostumbren demasiado a oirme hablar en español. Me costó mucha práctica y dudo que lo pudiera repetir igual! Disfruten con nuestro concierto!

Or in English—

Good evening! We are thrilled to be in Spain where there is still a team playing in the World Cup! This tour marks the end of the Turtle Creek Chorale's thirtieth anniversary season. In fact, this is the second time performing in Spain—the first being in 1995.

The repertoire you will hear this evening represents the variety of styles we perform at home. Each song on our program has very special meaning to us as a singing ensemble. We hope you enjoy the music we have grown to love so much.

Please do not get used to my speaking only in Spanish. This took a lot of practice and I'm not sure I can do it again! Enjoy and have fun!

Tour companies and local guides can be very helpful when securing translation assistance. Not only do you want to pronounce each word correctly in front of an audience of native speakers, but also you want to be sure you use the nomenclature of the region. In

Dallas, where the Spanish-speaking population is quite large, finding someone to translate the above passage into Spanish was an easy task; however, the Spanish spoken in Latin and South America does differ in subtle ways from that spoken in Spain. It would be wise for travelers to Spain to double check that their announcements are appropriate for that country and for that region. Extra points will always be given to those who use Catalan, not Castilian Spanish, when addressing an audience in Barcelona. The same theory applies to those traveling to Quebec City or Montreal, Canada.

WHAT REPERTOIRE HAVE YOU PERFORMED AND DO YOU RECOMMEND FOR THE ALL-MALE CHOIR?

Refer to Appendix F.

Programming concerts and selecting repertoire for your men's chorus is ultimately the same process as for a mixed chorus, though extra attention must be given to the various points addressed in this chapter. Gathering piles and piles of music—much of which will never be performed under your baton—is part of what we do as choral conductors. Program what you love; convey your passion for the music; and seize every opportunity to teach and impart musicianship to your singers. Rewards can be reaped at every step of the learning and performance process.

CHAPTER 8
AUDITIONS

Auditioning potential singers for your men's chorus is, in many ways, no different from those auditions you hold or have experienced yourself in a mixed-choir setting. Of course, the notable difference is the lack of women auditioning for the men's chorus—typically.

WHAT GENERAL PURPOSE DO AUDITIONS SERVE?

(JP) Auditions offer the conductor-teacher an opportunity to assess a singer's vocal character and general musicianship abilities. The skills evaluated, depending on what the audition entails, may include pitch matching, sight-singing, and knowledge of rhythm—both simple and complex. Measuring these aptitudes is considered normal for any audition, yet I find men who audition for male-only choirs do so in a slightly different manner from the way they do a mixed-chorus audition. Admittedly, I generalize greatly with this argument, and any supporting evidence is purely subjective, but observation has led me to believe that men auditioning for TTBB choirs do so with a certain sense of confidence and bravery.

One of the greatest reasons for joining a university glee club is camaraderie among men—the "Brothers, Sing On!" attitude. As such, many who audition do so with the enthusiastic encouragement of their peers. Inevitably, singers enter the audition room with a sense of boldness, and at times even a bit of entitlement. It is not difficult to explain this phenomenon if one acknowledges the "if he can get in I can get in" arrogance.

For high school boys, this assessment is perhaps not as accurate. High-schoolers desperately want to be part of a group, but they fear rejection and the potential for subsequent ostracism. The audition process is thus much scarier at this age and the possibility of failure prevents many from auditioning in the first place. In most instances, high school students possess much less of the wild enthusiasm often demonstrated by university students. For most of us who sang in a collegiate men's glee club, the chorus was in place of a fraternity or like organization. It was our brotherhood—our family away from home.

Nervousness also plays a role in virtually every audition. Singers who say they don't get nervous before and during an audition are probably lying. Fear of the unknown, fear of criticism, fear of judgment, fear of making a mistake, fear of failure, and fear of fear itself are all part of the normal audition process. When I walk into an audition, my desire to impress the adjudicators may not outweigh my fear of failing to impress them. Am I afraid of "crashing and burning" or am I afraid they just won't like me? What happens if I do my best and I still don't make the cut? What happens if I fail? What will happen WHEN I fail?

The internal monologue occurring at audition time is often overwhelming and can be truly deafening. Frequently, nervousness results in manufactured excuses, and I, as an adjudicator, can't stand singers who make excuses for their performance. "Sorry I messed up my prepared piece. I'm just so nervous." Or, "That sight-reading stunk. I have a cold. *Sniffle. Sniffle.*" There are thought processes one can put in place to alleviate such stresses.

As conductors and teachers, we must be consistent in our approach to auditioning. One way to do this is to announce and demonstrate the entire audition process well ahead of the actual audition date. Post a video online of a sample audition or put a DVD in the school or local library where a singer can view it on his own time. Set up a video camera in your office or classroom and record the entire audition from the moment he enters the room until the series of required tasks is complete and he exits. It's important to re-produce the tryout exactly as it will take place in real life. If a singer rehearses facing the window, be sure to have him face the window when the time comes. If a minute is allotted to review the sight-singing in silence, include that silent minute in your video, timing it to the second. Point out where the singer will stand during the audition and where you will be seated. Such details may seem ordinary, but for many, knowing exactly what to expect helps to alleviate some of the fear factor.

Some adjudicators may find the practice of publishing the audition method impractical, while others believe making the process public is, in essence, giving away the secret to the audition. Nevertheless, our goal should be to evaluate the singer's skills at his best, not while he's overcome with worry.

For specific ideas on what to listen for in your auditions, refer to the chapter titled "Parts and Placement."

It was stated earlier that only men audition for men's choirs, though as the world becomes more progressive, this is no longer true. The first time I learned of a woman auditioning for a TTBB ensemble was when I was in college. As my undergraduate institution is a public one and by law no campus club or organization can discriminate based on gender, every student received an opportunity to audition for the Men's Glee Club. While this was per-haps a first for the conductor and student leaders who scheduled the audition, the female student was told she would be administered the exact same audition as her male peers. If the timbre of her voice was consistent with that of the desired ensemble sound, then she would be accepted. If the timbre of her voice did not, then, as was the case for any male singer facing the same conclusion, she would be denied entry. In this instance, the female did audition but fell short of meeting the requirements for acceptance.

In recent years, the gay and lesbian choral movement has faced this situation with great respect for all people. I know of one all-male chorus in which both gender and gender identity were called into question during the audition and acceptance process. Gender, of course, is the distinction between male and female and there are many characteristics that determine one's gender assignment, including biological and physiological makeup. Gender identity, however, is the label (male or female) assigned to an individual based on one's sense of self.

In the gay men's chorus mentioned, the individual attended the first rehearsal and arrived for the audition as instructed. Dressed in men's clothing, this individual's facial and physical overall appearance clearly identified her as female.

WHAT DO YOU DO WHEN YOUR CHORUS IS A MEN'S CHORUS AND A FEMALE WANTS TO JOIN?

(JP) It is not uncommon to find female tenors singing in both church and community choirs. Women's voices lower with age and for many, the tenor part is often more suited than the alto. Furthermore, many church and community organizations lack tenors in their ensembles and the added support to the "men's" section is most welcome.

The gay and lesbian choral movement argues that vocal quality and musicianship remain most relevant and, as such, social and political agendas are secondary to the music-making. Never mind a chorus's mission statement, constitution, and bylaws; auditions are a time to determine if a voice meets the expectation of sound and if one's musicianship skills are at the requisite level.

AUDITIONS ARE FORMIDABLE. HOW CAN I MAKE THE PROCESS LESS SCARY FOR MY SINGERS?

(Diane Loomer) There are many ways to make the audition a less frightening, more positive prospect, especially if the purpose is to be inclusive rather than exclusive, or where you are trying to encourage rather than discourage prospective singers from join-ing a choir. Some of these suggestions are so obvious they probably don't need to be included, yet I've seen many audition situations where these considerations weren't thought of ahead of time.

1. Any singer wanting to audition for my men's choir or my mixed choir is always asked to first attend a rehearsal and observe and listen to the choir rehearsing. I find that this experience accurately informs the prospective singer of the skills needed to sing in the choir, the level of the choir's singing, and basically what we're all about.

2. At the audition, I have someone with a positive and outgoing personality watching for, greeting, and welcoming the auditioning singer, thereby helping to put him at ease.

3. The physical setting should have lots of light, plenty of room, and fresh air. There should be chairs in case the singer needs to sit and, of course, water should be available. It becomes a more welcoming environment if the audition process begins with a brief sit-down conversation between auditioner and auditionee. Topics discussed might include the singer's musical interests, education, and performing background.

4. When auditioning inexperienced singers, I usually play for the audition myself. There's nothing more frightening for a timid or inexperienced singer than to walk into a room and see not one, but two or three "formidable experts" waiting to hear him sing.

5. If more than one person is in the room to hear the audition, be sure the prospective singer is warned of that possibility well ahead of time, knows why the extra people are there, and is comfortable with that reasoning.

6. A music stand should be set up for the singer.

7. When possible, the prospective singer should be sent ahead of time a schedule of rehearsals and concerts and a statement of the choir's policies regarding attendance, financial involvement, dues, concert attire, etc.

8. Confidentiality and trust are essential ingredients throughout the audition. Do whatever you can to assure your singer that those conditions are integral to and guaranteed in the process.

9. I often ask my section leaders to sit in on new-member auditions, but I make sure the auditioning singer knows this well ahead of time and is comfortable with that scenario. Having section leaders present helps me (and ultimately the choir) in many ways. When singers are accepted, the section leaders know something—sound, experience, etc.—about the people coming into their sections. If a singer's acceptance into the choir is questionable, the section leaders gladly provide their thoughts and wisdom.

If I want to hear the possibility of blend or no blend, having the section leaders there is a perfect opportunity to put the singer into a quartet situation.

WHAT ARE YOU TRYING TO ASSESS WHEN AUDITIONING POTENTIAL NEW MEMBERS?

(Derrick Brookins) Although I assess several things when auditioning a young singer, there are two main items—pitch accuracy and melodic recollection. For the first, I instruct the student to perform a simple vocal scale from *do* to *sol*. I demonstrate how I'd like this sung using proper posture, breath, and well-rounded vowels. This exercise is performed in several keys and allows me to check the singer's ability to match simple pitch and perform a melodic line, albeit only an ascending scale. I also notice if he mimics my posture, etc. Then, I play a short melodic line on the piano and ask the student to sing it back to me on a neutral syllable, such as *la* or *noo*. This allows me to check his musical ear and test his pitch memory.

Surprisingly, I do not require singers to bring in a prepared piece. I don't find it useful and it often turns my auditions into something similar to those pop singing contests seen on television. Instead, each singer is asked to perform *America* (*My Country 'Tis of Thee*). They're asked to duplicate this in at least six keys, allowing me to check vocal flexibility, range, and agility. In some cases, it teaches the student an American patriotic song. I am always surprised to learn just how many students don't know the words to this song!

One of the most revealing aspects used in my typical audition process is something I saw done by Dr. Anton Armstrong of St. Olaf College. He asked each singer to recite a short poem in his or her best performance voice. Simply reading aloud demonstrates the singer's aptitude for speech clarity, inflection, theatrical ability, and projection. With this exercise, I have been able to diagnose speech impediments, hearing loss, and even alternative learning styles.

The recitation I use is extracted from William Shakespeare's play *Richard III* (1594):

Now is the winter of our discontent
Made glorious summer by this sun of York;
And all the clouds that lour'd upon our house
In the deep bosom of the ocean buried.
Now are our brows bound with victorious wreaths;
Our bruised arms hung up for monuments;
Our stern alarums chang'd to merry meetings,
Our dreadful marches to delightful measures.
Grim-visag'd war hath smooth'd his wrinkled front;
And now—instead of mounting barbed steeds

To fright the souls of fearful adversaries—
He capers nimbly in a lady's chamber
To the lascivious pleasing of a lute.

What are your key assessment points of each new-member audition?

(Diane Loomer) Whether I'm auditioning a potential member for a volunteer community choir or an experienced singer for a professional choir, I listen and look for the following:

- Voice quality and tone

- Vocal range

- Pitch accuracy

- Sight-reading ability

- Language aptitude

- General acumen level

- Blending ability

- Ability to sing softly and maintain pitch and quality

- Alertness and personality

- Ability to follow instructions

- Musical, vocal, and choral experience

- Ability to quickly correct mistakes

- Vocal problems such as wobble, excessive vibrato, or roughness in sound

- Attitude

- Eyes, face, and breathing pattern while singing

Please describe, in detail, how you organize a typical audition.

(Diane Loomer) Each audition begins with an informal chat to put the singer at ease, explore his personality, and find out more about his musical experience. Next, I take the singer through a series of free-singing exercises to evaluate the voice quality, pitch accuracy, vocal range, and "intelligence level." What I am really listening for is his most natural voice. I ask him to sing in both his chest and his head voice. The sound of the head voice tells me so much about his ability to sing in the upper range without straining the voice or pressing the sound. I also assess variations and abnormalities in the vocal tone, the ability to modify and control the upper register, pitch accuracy in both the high and low range, and whether the voice will contribute to or detract from the overall sound of the choir.

Auditions should also help reveal how well the singer follows verbal instruction. Does he have a good sense of his own voice and can he accurately match a pitch demonstrated by a singer or played on the piano? How quickly can the singer echo a melody or note sequence? These are all skills to be evaluated in one's initial hearing.

I then ask him to sing a piece of music of his own choosing—one he feels shows his most comfortable and natural singing voice. If he doesn't have a song prepared, I suggest a well-known tune such as *Somewhere Over the Rainbow*, *Silent Night*, or perhaps his national anthem. Such a demonstration can tell you a lot in a very few notes. I tend to be wary of those who have done only solo work and sing in a "solo style"—with lots of vibrato and/or volume, or a pushed, pressed, or false sound. It's exciting to learn whether he can sing musically, with good phrasing and dynamic variation. It also tells me where his most comfortable range is.

I next have each singer do a bit of sight-reading. I start with a fairly easy piece and give him quite a bit of help on the piano if he needs it. If he does well, I'll try a second, tougher piece with fewer piano cues.

I also check listening ability and, if relevant, familiarity with music theory. For example, I might play a major or minor triad and ask him to sing all the notes he hears. Some may be able to sing only the top note or the bottom note, but some will impress by singing all three notes in ascending order. I also ask a singer if he knows the chord quality—major or minor. If he finds this simple, I'll make the listening examples more difficult (diminished, augmented, tonal cluster chords, etc.) and ask him to sing the notes he hears, as well as to identify the chords. I may also ask the individual to identify a key signature by looking at the number of flats and sharps or to explain the time signature.

To gauge "choral chops" and experience, I present singers with a short list of composers. I then show a few musical excerpts and ask the singer to match the excerpt to the composer. The text, in its original language, is included, but the composer's name has been removed. Even if he may not know or recognize the musical quotation, he is asked to try to match the excerpt with the composer. This part of the audition gives me an idea of the singer's "quickness in deductive thought," as well as his choral experience and knowledge. Often, I include reading as part of the audition process. Singers are asked to read a familiar, short phrase in German, Italian, French, Spanish, and Latin. This might include *Credo in unum Deum* or *Guten Tag*. This tests pronunciation skill as well as language knowledge.

Again, it gives me a feel for "quickness" and musicality. I find that how people read is often how they'll sing!

Finally, if I have the luxury of other people helping me listen to each audition, I ask the auditionee to excuse us for a few minutes while we discuss what we've heard. Whether or not I have other people listening with me, I try to let the person auditioning know immediately of my final decision and, more important, what I've heard. If the singer isn't accepted, I suggest other choirs in the city that may suit him better. In the case of the voluntary community singer, my decision comes as an immediate acceptance: "You're welcome to join the choir. Can you start with our next rehearsal?" My decision may be a conditional one: "I think you have good potential, but because of your inexperience, I would like you to start on a trial basis." In the second instance, I always assign one of the trusted section leaders to sit next to the new singer in rehearsal. If it is clear to the section leader that the singer is simply not working into the choral situation for whatever reason, I make time to talk with him about it and how we might best move forward.

As onerous as it may seem, reauditioning every few years is a necessary and helpful process to determine where singers are in learning and developing vocal skills and whether they've been placed properly according to voice part.

Obviously, I place quite a bit of emphasis on the singer's teachability and quickness. Especially in a men's choir, I often get prospective singers who do not possess a great deal of singing experience and musical knowledge. I find, however, that if a singer has good pitch and a natural sound and is quick to catch on, then, most often, he does better than someone with lots of experience and his own idea of what the sound should be.

Each audition takes roughly twenty to twenty-five minutes.

CHAPTER 9
WARM-UPS

Warm-ups are something we all did as students, do today as directors, and will likely do throughout our careers. Most conductors do the same warm-ups with every chorus they direct, regardless of size, voice classification, level, or time of year. It is only the professional ensemble conductor that expects singers to arrive prepared, vocally and mentally, ready to make music without a moment of warm-up time. I witnessed the Chicago Symphony Chorus start many a rehearsal without a warm-up. But when I was among the singers in the Cleveland Orchestra Chorus, my fellow singers and I always took time to focus both our minds and our instruments at the start of each rehearsal and performance.

For many reasons, I place great value on warm-up time at the start of each rehearsal. Like athletes, we want to stretch, tone, and activate our bodies before we put them through their paces. Warm-up time is also when we focus on the specific techniques of our "sport" that may creep up on us later in the rehearsal. Think of it this way: A tennis player is attempting to refine his serve. Specifically, his left-hand vertical ball toss is weak. Rather than practice this technique during the match, the player arrives early to stretch his arms and shoulders, review the order of movements for the serve, and repeat the ball toss over and over until the technique is honed. For the choral artist, warm-ups are the perfect time to practice those techniques used on the "court."

Warm-ups, however, if simply for the sake of warm-ups and without specific goals, are highly undesirable. A conductor must be able to substantiate and convey the relevance of each and every warm-up and singers must take this time seriously. Remember, more often than not, a choir conductor is the *only* voice teacher a chorister will have. It is imperative to explain the purpose and describe the proper technique for singing each warm-up exercise.

Countless resources are available to help conductors discover and create productive warm-ups, but targeting those that activate the mind, body, and instrument of male singers is a challenge. Let me offer a few scenarios and useful warm-ups.

Note: These are not complete warm-up sequences.

Varsity Men's Choir; 11th- and 12th-graders only
It's Monday after prom and four days before the final concert of the year.
Period A—7:50 a.m.
It's going to be a tough rehearsal.
The boys are tired and unfocused.

1.   Physical activity is a must. Employ the "layup (or jump shot) with follow-through" exercise. Begin by having the chorus stand and spread out at arm's length. To start, place the imaginary basket at eye level. I won't describe here how to actually do a layup, as I have about as much athletic ability as a three-legged bulldog; instead, I recommend viewing such techniques on the Internet. Better yet, invite the head basketball coach into your rehearsal to demonstrate the technique to your boys! His or her presence would certainly be a surprise for your singers and, in just minutes, the energy of this early-morning rehearsal would be exactly where you want it to be—HIGH.

     Shoot the basket at eye level first, then increase the height of the imaginary basket to six feet. This will require singers to reach above their heads. Be sure to emphasize the "follow-through," where the hand freely goes up and over without tension or interference. Remind singers how this maneuver mimics the flow of air and the desired height of the soft palate. Involve the entire body by making the imaginary hoop appear at regulation height—ten feet. This will require singers to jump as well as follow through. Bear in mind, it's 7:50 a.m. and your singers are becoming fully engaged.

2.   With bodies warmed up, we can now address the voice. High school boys, like adults, certainly have "morning voice." (Refer to the chapter titled "Anatomy of the Male Voice" for an explanation of this phenomenon.) It's best not to tackle the upper register at the outset when boys are just starting their day. Use this time wisely, so begin by reviewing a technically difficult passage not in the upper part of the tessitura.

     Finding the core in the lower register may be your goal for this warm-up. On neutral syllables, such as *loo-ah*, begin in E-flat major. Sing a simple five-note descending scale (*loo-ah* on each note of the scale). Lowering by half step upon each repeat, carry the core of the highest note downward while freeing any weight or muscle engagement that wants so desperately to creep into the sound on the lower notes. High school boys often want to power these low notes, but the sound is typically unfocused, has no resonance, and lacks substantial projection. Instead, as pitches descend, singers should modify from [a] to [ɔ] keeping the soft palate lifted and the core of the sound forward. It is smart to repeatedly relate the physical look of the layup to the placement of the soft palate, as these connections are easily made but quickly forgotten by younger singers.

3. Slowly warm up the upper register using an ascending arpeggio—*do mi sol mi do* starting in D major. I use the syllables *No-e-o-e-o,* keeping both vowels closed. Singers tend to spread these particular vowels, making for an ugly *Noh-wee-oh-wee-oh* sound. Placing the index finger of each hand at the corners of the mouth is a useful reminder to keep the aperture taut and the vowels aligned. The exercise should ascend high enough that the first tenors feel the stretch—perhaps to C major with a G on top—but remember: this isn't a warm-up for the falsetto register. On the descent, keep the boys' ears alert by leaping down a minor third or moving up by a whole step. Singers expect to descend by half step in such a simple exercise, so practice active listening! A little musical humor early in the morning is never a bad thing.

Community Men's Choir
50 singers
7:00 p.m. rehearsal
The concert opener needs the most work and you aim to create a majestic sound without being forced.

It's important to understand that vowels play a huge role in so much more than clarity of text. Vowels affect tone color, intonation, and dynamic control. In this scenario, we want to harness a "manly" sound by singing with great energy while modifying and maintaining pure vowels.

ee - ee,   ee - eh,   ee - aw. _____

With regard to vowel modification, in this warm-up I remind singers to bring the bottom lip forward while singing *ee,* to lift the soft palate on *eh,* and to drop the jaw while keeping a tall, rounded, beautiful *aw* through the octave leap. To engage the body, I ask my men to *plié* like a ballet dancer—dip at the knees and fan the arms out (hands begin together in front of the hips and gently spread out to "hug a whiskey barrel"). Yes, this usually elicits a laugh, but the exercise enables singers to use their bodies in support of their singing. This exercise is a lively one and should be sung *forte.*

College Glee Club

International tour

Gothic cathedral

Live acoustic

Start of a quick warm-up prior to the performance

1. In a situation like this, it is important to provide singers with an opportunity to experience their sound at each extreme. How soft can we sing and still be heard in the back of the room? What does it take to fill the room with sound? What is too much sound? Where do consonants need to fall?

    A new concert space is always exciting and every ensemble will need time to focus and tune their ears. It is very easy to gaze at the ceiling embellishments, examine the organ pipes, and watch chaperones get situated. Anyone who has toured with an ensemble knows exactly how this feels. Begin with a calming warm-up. Most of my rehearsals begin with humming, but this becomes even more important in a situation like this one.

    "Yawn on the inside; remember the dome. Close your eyes and sing with the joy of being in a new and wonderful concert venue. Men, use your falsetto freely and gently. Don't let me hear you flip. As the warm-up gets higher in register, move from a hum to an *oo*, then to *oh*, *eh*, and finally *aw*. Stay controlled. Listen to your neighbor. Hear the ensemble. Hear the reverberation. Internalize the history of this church." That last comment always encourages the singer to be present in the moment. When we are present, we are aware, and when we are aware, we are focused. "Let's sing!" Repeat the exercise ascending by half step.

2. The exercise below encourages tall vowels, great diaphragmatic support, and full singing. There are many phrases that fit this warm-up, so be creative and vary them often. I like the following:

Sing with vigor and strength and remind singers to modify those pesky diphthongs! The words "how," "wide," and "sky" should sung beautifully. Men have a tendency to force the descending arpeggio, so offer the image of a "rising hot air balloon" to model the desired sound and palate position. The vocal mechanism should remain in a lifted place even as the notes themselves descend.

3. While it's possible to move directly into repertoire at this point in the rehearsal, clarity and placement of diction may be worth reviewing in a setting like this. Warm-ups are the perfect time to practice this technique.

    Here is a simple, fun exercise that requires no notes be sung yet works well to unify singers' consonants.

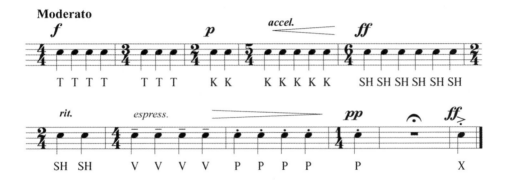

Improvise this entire exercise varying tempo, dynamic indication (size of gesture), and style of each beat or series of beats. Insist that the ensemble focus on the conductor or warm-up leader. Often, mistakes are made at the outset of this exercise when singers are still tuning in. It is inevitable that one or two singers will make a glaring mistake or have a "solo," resulting in laughter by everyone. It's always an amusing warm-up.

Conductors should use this exercise to review consonant shape and the position of the resonance chamber that support these sounds. For example, is it your preference for the *T* to be *tih* or *tuh*? Do you prefer a slight horizontal smile or a vertical dropped jaw behind the lips? The answers to such questions can easily be reviewed during this particular warm-up exercise.

Note: If you looked carefully at the musical example above, you noticed an oddity—the letter X. Remember, a little humor in the rehearsal is a good thing! Try it out on your singers and watch them break into laughter when they realize they don't know what to say when you call out, "Now do it on X!"

PLEASE OUTLINE YOUR "TYPICAL" WARM-UP WHEN WORKING WITH MEN'S CHOIRS. IS THERE A STANDARD ORDER OF ACTIVITIES AND WHAT ARE SOME OF THE ACTUAL WARM-UPS YOU USE?

(Jerry Blackstone) I loathe wasting precious rehearsal time in needless warm-up exercises. If there are specific musical and physical needs that can be improved during those first few minutes of rehearsal, however, then the warm-up should be shaped to fit those unique needs. We might need to improve breath management, physical engagement, posture issues, pitch sensitivity, vowel color and unity, articulation possibilities, range extension, falsetto engagement, *passaggio* management, dynamic variation, "follow the conductor" issues, and group camaraderie building. Each group, whether a university male chorus, a festival group, a high school group, or an older group, will have its own specific challenges that will shape the warm-up. Warm-up periods longer than five minutes should be the exception rather than the norm.

1. To address group camaraderie, I tend to begin the rehearsal with back rubs or some sort of physical exercise, such as jumping jacks, jogging around the hallways or outside, or a short exercise regimen (depending on the time of the rehearsal—mornings need more, evenings, less). With young singers, this might be the time to engage their rhythmic energy by doing some imitation exercises.

2. Using the high speaking voice (the "chant" voice), we might speak consonants on each beat while the conductor changes tempo, meter, and dynamic levels. This develops a sense of breath energy, trains follow-the-conductor skills, and helps singers identify their floaty head voice, a technique that is very helpful in developing beautiful vowels and diction sensitivity.

3. Five-note descending figures tend to work best with male singers, carrying the upper voice down rather than carrying the lower voice up. At this point in the warm-up, *my, my, my, my, my* or *boy, boy, boy, boy, boy* or *noh, noh, noh, noh, noh* (all on the descending five-note scale) will work well to keep the sound forward, engage the breath, develop resonance, and finesse over the *passaggio*. These should be done *mf* with a sense of *diminuendo* from 5 through 1. This mantra, "The last note is the softest, the sweetest, the warmest, the most beautiful," helps to remind singers that musicality must be present in every note and phrase they sing.

4. Next, we might go to *snah* (5, 4), *snee* (3, 2), *snoo* (1), engendering a sweeter, more lyric sound, still emphasizing that "the last note is the softest, the sweetest, the warmest,

the most beautiful." Begin each repetition a half step higher, ascending to the falsetto range, perhaps as high as high E or F (more than an octave above middle C), and high enough to require all singers to sing in a ringing falsetto. No one should be allowed to sing an octave lower and conductor demonstrations can be very helpful. Start this exercise on A below middle C and ascend to the top E; then descend (still 5, 4, 3, 2, 1), expecting the men to shift to "regular" voice whenever they wish, but without a bump ("Don't let me hear you when you change"). Shift easily, elegantly, like driving a stick-shift transmission without any sense of "clunk" when shifting from falsetto to chest voice. "Lighten up" or "lift over the shift" or "float over the shift" are good analogies.

5. On *snoo* (1, 2, 3, 2, 1), beginning on G-flat above middle C, and beginning each repetition a half step lower, the group will begin in falsetto and finesse the shift to chest voice at differing pitch levels, depending on the sections. It is a good idea to alert the T1's to "be ready to shift" around E or F, T2's be ready to shift at about the same time, B1's be ready to shift around E or E-flat, etc. End when the upper note of the three-note figure is on the A below middle C.

6. It is now time to unify vowels.

Begin with an *oo* vowel on A (220 Hz) and unify it using the index finger to circle the lips. EVERYONE must do this, not just the conductor.

Unify *oh* by making a circle between the thumb and middle finger of the right hand (as if wrapping your hand around a pipe) and instruct singers to focus the sound through that opening—about eighteen inches in front of the lips. (EVERYONE must do this.)

Unify *ee* by pointing all of the fingers of both hands toward the ceiling, in front of the face, with palms parallel to each other, as if on the sides of a pillar. Sing the *ee* between the hands; tilt the hands back toward parallel to the ceiling, and hear how ugly and spread it becomes. Return the hands to the tall position and the desired sound. Beautiful *ee*'s are tall and natural, not wide and spread or dark and covered.

Unify *ah* by placing the right hand at eye level, palm toward floor, and the left hand at belt level or lower, palm toward ceiling. Imagine the sound tall and warm with lots of "north" and some "south."

Unify *eh* by stretching an imaginary rubber band with the thumb of the right hand from the bridge of your nose. The *eh* is "north" not "south" and is narrow, not wide and down.

All of this can be done in five to seven minutes and the conductor has established musicality, vowel standards, focus, energy, and rehearsal sensitivity. Now, REHEARSE!

(Jefferson Johnson) My initial goal is to get their attention in a way that is musical. A fast pace and a stern demeanor are important during these initial activities. The tone we want to set is not one of "enjoyable work." The goal is to turn attention into concentration as quickly as possible.

To do this, I use a variety of attention-getting exercises.

Echo claps

I clap a 4-beat pattern and the choir repeats.

Mirrored movements

The conductor does a variety of arm gestures and the choir mirrors. Moving both arms together is the easiest level. Advance to one arm kept stationary while the other moves. Hardest level: Each arm moves independently.

Same movements in canon

The choir repeats the conductor's gestures in a continuous canon at various rhythmic intervals; for example, "Do what I do but start one beat later." This canonic idea also works with both clapping and echo exercises as described above.

Conducting patterns

I conduct a series of patterns (4/4, 3/4, 2/4, etc.) and have the choir clap on certain beats. For example, "Clap on every second beat." I alternate tempi and show dynamic contrast and expect singers to respond accordingly.

The second stage of the warm-up is a focus on posture and breathing.

Posture

I prefer to set the posture from the top down. Singers raise both arms above their heads ("touchdown at the Super Bowl") and slowly lower them without moving the chest. Then we "pull a string tied to the top of our head" making us "a half inch taller."

BREATHING

Here are some of my favorites: "Pretend that you have a hole in your throat. Breathe in through the hole and exhale by blowing a cooling breath over a bowl of hot soup." Also, "Sit on the edge of your chair with your elbows on your knees. Inhale. Relax. Memorize the sensation of breathing in this position. Now, stand and try breathing in the same way."

At this point, we are ready to vocalize. Always perform these exercises unaccompanied if possible.

TONE (VOWELS)

I start with unison humming on a descending five-note scale beginning in C-sharp major: *sol fa mi re do.* Then repeat up by half steps. When we get to F-sharp major, I ask them to hold these notes on the way down: T1 on *sol*, T2 on *mi*, B1 on *re*, and B2 on *do*. This creates a major ninth chord. Holding this chord, we form the five Latin vowels: *ah, eh, ee, aw* (but I prefer *oh*), and *softly* on *oo*. Every vowel is accompanied by a specific hand sign—a mandatory gesture[10] done by every choir member. These are not optional!

HEAD VOICE

The head voice is accessed using the same five-note unison exercise listed above starting in [high] E major (and sometimes minor) on a very closed and round *noo noo noo noo noo*. With each repetition, descend by half steps until singers are mixing the head and chest registers. Statements such as "Bring the head voice down, gentlemen" and "Maintain the head quality as long as possible" are both effective.

INTONATION

I find intonation to be the biggest challenge for male choirs.

Adapted from a Robert Shaw technique, on a unison G-natural (*oo* vowel, *pp* dynamic) the choir slides up a half step in unison over 8 slow counts. All singers trace the pitch by moving their index finger up approximately 8 inches. The goal is to move exactly together and evenly across the huge distance we call a "half step." Then, try descending over 8 counts. This tends to be even more difficult. Adding counts (from 8 to 12, 16, etc.)

---

10   Research has shown that when every member of a choir does a kinesthetic gesture while singing, learning is optimized. This relates to the theory of Learning Styles, which recognizes that our choirs consist of visual, auditory, and kinesthetic learners. Every time a warm-up or rehearsal technique involves a gesture by the singers, we are addressing all three learning styles simultaneously, thus maximizing the efficiency of the technique.

increases the challenge. Finally (perhaps later in the school year), do the same series of exercises but on a *staccato doot* instead of on the *legato oo*. The *staccato* is more difficult but yields the best results as it relates best to real pieces. I recommend doing these exercises (in some form) every rehearsal.

RANGE EXTENSION

For the upper range, I employ a variety of triad- and arpeggio-based ascending exercises in unison on open vowels.

Start in the middle range—maybe B-flat major. As singers ascend above the treble clef staff, remind them to modify the open vowel, perhaps *ah* or *eh*, toward a more closed vowel; for example, *ah* becomes more like *oh*, *eh* has more pucker, etc. Encourage singers to "mix in the head voice" sooner rather than later.

For lower range extension, I use a unison, descending slide on an open vowel (*ah* or *eh*) from *sol* to *do*, starting midrange and descending by half steps for each repetition. Make sure young singers don't tuck the chin or "reach" for the low notes.

HARMONY

Sing a B-major scale (using solfège) ascending and descending in a four-part canon at various intervals. Conductor holds any given pitch at any moment ("Tune it" or "Listen"), then proceeds to the final unison tonic. Repeat up by half step for a couple of repetitions. Choose starting intervals that will appear in the music for that day (for example, major seconds or major thirds). Also, vary the order in which voice parts enter. Sometimes the baritones will begin followed by the seconds, the firsts, and then the basses. Other times I begin with the firsts and add at random. Incorporate minor scales as desired. Start with two-part divisi if necessary and work your way up to four parts. The important thing is to ensure success.

ARE THERE WARM-UPS THAT TARGET THE FALSETTO WELL?

(Matthew Oltman) By and large, males who sing primarily in falsetto voice use the same vocalises and technical exercises that any other singer, male or female, uses. The falsetto voice requires all the same physical skills as any of the more common voice types do: breath support, placement, body alignment, and relaxed jaw, neck, and tongue.

It is hard to say that specific exercises would somehow be particularly applicable to countertenors; exercises that are good for baritones or sopranos, say, are good for countertenors, too, and vice versa. Exercising the falsetto is an integral part of vocalizing for all voice types. It is, after all, an important part of the male voice and should not be ignored.

Exercises such as "sirens" (starting at the very bottom of one's range and sliding all the way up to the very top and sliding back down again) are good ways to awaken the entire voice and can help bridge the gap between the modal voice and the falsetto. Exercises that work on the onset of phonation, while being valuable throughout one's range, are particularly helpful in the falsetto, as a clean onset can be more challenging.

An example of this type of exercise might be to sing four *staccato* notes on the vowel *oo* in the middle of one's falsetto range followed by a five-note descending scale. Careful attention should be paid to the accuracy of the repeated pitches as well as to the gentleness and cleanness of the onset, avoiding unwanted accents that often distort the pitch.

WHAT WARM-UPS WORK BEST FOR ADOLESCENT MALE VOICES?

Refer to the chapter titled "The Adolescent Male Voice: Categorization to Maturation."

CHAPTER 10
SIGHT-SINGING

Sight-singing is irrefutably the most intimidating and frightening of all the musical proficiencies in which singers, choristers, and conductors are expected to excel. Ask a singer to compare sight-singing with an instrumentalist's sight-reading and you will receive an earful. The argument goes something like this: When a clarinetist covers the correct holes at the correct time it is assumed the pitch and timing of that pitch will be correct. A singer will tell you that an instrumentalist doesn't have to pick pitches out of thin air. This is the argument, legitimate or not, made by us singers.

While many find validity in this claim, most do understand that sight-singing is not at all an ability to "pick pitches out of thin air." Rather, sight-singing is a methodical practice whereby one pitch has a direct and obvious relationship to another. Frankly, defined in such a simple way, sight-singing should be an easy task of recognizing those specific pitch relationships and performing them accurately. If only it were that painless.

To teach beginning musicians of any age to sight-sing is a daunting task, and I'll freely add that most do not enjoy this part of the job, but why is it such a challenge?

1. Students don't want to practice sight-singing during class.

2. Students despise sight-singing homework and rarely approach it using the instructions and methods provided.

3. Students often think sight-singing is wasted time. Their mindset is one of, "Play it on the piano and I'll sing it back to you. What's wrong with doing it that way?"

4. Teachers don't like to give up valuable rehearsal time that could be spent on concert or contest repertoire.

5. Appropriate resources and quality teaching aids are difficult to find.

6. Teaching sight-singing requires daily preparation and lesson planning by the teacher.

7. Success is not immediate.

Sight-singing *is* difficult to do correctly. As such, negativity stemming from the fear of failure is common; therefore, finding the positives inherent in the learning process is vital to success. How, then, do we teach it to our men?

The best and most effective way to teach sight-singing to your men requires a three-fold approach:

1. Be consistent. With my high school choruses, I use the analogy of weight lifting. It may be a gross generalization, but most young men understand that to increase strength and muscle size you have to work out every day or every other day. Going to the weight room every Monday (and only on Mondays) will result in little growth and constant soreness. Muscle development happens when you "hit it" regularly.

2. Be structured. Using the same analogy, weight lifters create and stick with a program for a period of time. For example, Mondays and Thursdays are chest and triceps days. On each of these days (week after week), the individual performs three sets of three different exercises for a total of nine drills. Growth will be imminent! Apply this notion of structure and consistency to your sight-singing pedagogy and, as was said about weight lifting, growth will be imminent!

3. Be creative. Insisting something be fun that is not inherently fun will not work. Ever tell a joke and receive nothing but blank stares in return? This is essentially what happens when you force "fun" sight-singing activities on your singers. Instead, variety and creativity in teaching are the keys. The simplest melodic passage can be transformed into any number of great sight-singing exercises for your men's choir. *Twinkle, Twinkle, Little Star*, for example, is made more interesting with the addition of a vocal beat box. Invite one student to provide vocal percussion, as backup to the melody.

Traditional Melody

Perform this exercise first in a major key using solfège and then repeat it with the third lowered (in the key of C major, E becomes E-flat or *mi* becomes *me*). Repeat using a lowered sixth.

Using the same melody, provide notation for various rhythms and performance styles. Take this opportunity to practice more than just notes and rhythms—practice making real music!

Don't consider this melody to be a legitimate one? Even Mozart, at the age of 25, used the *Twinkle, Twinkle* tune in his Twelve Variations on *Ah vous dirai-je, Manan* (K. 265/300e).

Example with Lowered Third and Various Markings

Vocal Percussion

Doom ti-ki tsee ti-ki Doom ti-ki tsee ti-ki Doom ti-ki tsee Brrr Doom ti-ki tsee ti-ki.

Learning to sight-sing can be boring and tedious, though it doesn't have to be. We may never be called "cool" by using this approach, but boring and tedious are deadly adjectives when introducing choristers to the art of sight-singing.

DO YOU ASSESS RHYTHM SKILLS AND SIGHT-SINGING ABILITIES THROUGHOUT THE YEAR? IF SO, HOW?

(Peter Bagley) General musicianship skills are first determined at the beginning of the academic or concert season via the private audition. Rhythm and sight-singing skills are not specifically segregated at this time. Greater priority is given to excellent listening and concentration skills. Call-back auditions for all applicants in each voice part are held at the conclusion of the private solo audition to determine how well the applicant listens, understands, and adjusts to singers of his voice part.

(Derrick Brookins) Yes. I always begin the year by having each member of the choir perform a weekly sight-singing (eight-measure) quiz, ranging from intermediate to advanced levels. The choir prepares and competes each spring in the annual UIL (University Interscholastic League) concert and sight-singing portion.

WHAT SPECIAL METHODS DO YOU EMPLOY FOR TEACHING ADOLESCENT BOYS (MIDDLE SCHOOL) TO SIGHT-SING?

(Kari Gilbertson) The key to teaching middle school boys to sight-read is range. However, the most difficult thing to manage with a middle school choir is that the many ranges preclude everyone from sight-reading in harmony. Furthermore, students must develop the skills necessary to sight-sing a single line before they are able to sight-sing in multiple parts. The practical thing, then, is to start with rhythm for all of the boys. When beginning to read melodic lines, we sing in a range where even the highest tenor can reach the lowest note. It is the responsibility and skill of the baritones to sing in a higher and lighter range until we can develop some pitch practice on melodic contour. I often say to my students, "With great range comes great responsibility." After we successfully sing single melodic lines, we move to combinable lines and parallel lines so the tenor II's and baritones can develop muscle memory in their specific range.

When we begin to sing more homophonic/chordal music, I think it is important that each section know where it fits in the chord and what its responsibility in the chord function is. The best way I have found to do this is to make the sight-reading sections analogous to the "special teams" on a football team. My John Madden-like playbook descriptions are:

- Basses are "*Do* and all things below."

- Tenor II's are "*Mi* and all things around it."

- Tenor I's are generally "*Sol* and all things great and beautiful nearby."

This silly and humorous analogy seems to help boys realize that each section manages a different part of the playbook. In fact, novice three-part sight-reading is, in essence, formulated on these three rules of our "TTB Sight-Reading Playbook."

DO YOU WRITE YOUR OWN EXERCISES OR USE A PRESCRIBED METHODOLOGY?

(Derrick Brookins) To teach sight-singing to individual singers, I use the textbook *90 Days to Sight Reading Success* by Stan McGill and H. Morris Stevens, Jr. (Alliance Music Publishing, AMC2010). With regard to teaching sight-reading in the choral setting, I use UIL men's sight-reading literature from previous year's state lists.

DO YOU TEACH SIGHT-SINGING TO YOUR MEN THE SAME WAY YOU DO WITH YOUR MIXED CHOIR?

(Ethan Sperry) To me, sight-reading is sight-reading. The skills you are teaching are the same regardless of who is in the room. If the book you use has no TTBB or TB examples, transpose some. Have some of the tenors sing the women's parts down an octave. This creates a different voicing from what the composer intended, but is still a good exercise. If you don't want your men singing in the wrong clef or in lines that are out of order, I suggest you recopy the example (in the transposed version) to your blackboard. I have actually performed many SATB works with my TTBB chorus just by doing this. The pattern usually remains: T1's sing the soprano line down an octave, the T2's sing the tenor as written, the baritones sing the alto down an octave, and the basses remain on the written bass line. One of my favorite published pieces for TTBB is K. Lee Scott's version of Faure's *Cantique de Jean Racine* (Hinshaw Music, Inc. HMC714), and all he did to Faure's original is exactly what I describe above. I actually like it more than the SATB original.

WHAT PRINTED RESOURCES ARE CURRENTLY AVAILABLE FOR TEACHING SIGHT-SINGING?

Refer to Appendix B.

CHAPTER 11
RECRUITING

In 1990, the Indiana Music Educators Association, along with the Wabash College Glee Club and then-director Nina Gilbert, offered an interest session titled "Attracting Men to Your Choral Organization." The discussion covered several major areas necessary for successful recruiting and provides an ideal structure that I have adapted for the beginning topics in this chapter.

CREATING AN IMAGE

Perception. Being "cool" is a tricky thing to do. Staying cool (and current) is even trickier. Think of it this way—you see a new, shiny, red convertible car. Your buddy, who happens to be your age, is at the wheel. No doubt, you think he is cool for having such a hot car. The same car pulls up a day later, only this time it is a man your grandfather's age driving. No doubt, you view him as less cool. Same car—cool for some, yet lesser so for others.

It is no secret: those perceived "cool" are your best recruiters, at both the high school and university levels. These are the individuals who tend to be outgoing and ready to take risks. These are typically the singers who are willing to wear the fun costumes, put their heart and soul into choreography, and make singing fun for those inherently less gregarious. Having outgoing, affable men in leadership positions makes others want to participate in choir.

Image is more than just who is in the ensemble. Image is dependent on what an ensemble does and how others perceive it. Choosing appropriate repertoire is vital to creating the kind of image you wish for your men's ensemble. A song such as *Rainbow 'Round My Shoulder,* arranged by Robert DeCormier for TTBB choir and small percussion (Lawson-Gould Publishing, LG51757), is definitely a "manly song." This chain-gang tune encourages boys to stick out their chests and sing with gusto. Choreography is easily created for this tune and costumes would be inexpensive and easily made. The addition of onomatopoeic percussion (chains, brake drums, etc.) completes this performance and makes it a suitable piece for young men to sing. Remember: guys, especially younger ones, want masculine parts to sing!

Lettering. In most high schools, varsity athletics play an important role in creating school spirit. One tangible item associated with being the best is the varsity letter. Having a varsity letter associated with your choral program encourages students to join choir and remain involved until they earn this coveted honor. To use the all-important word once again, be sure the design of your varsity letter is "cool."

Collaboration. Offering opportunities for your high school boys to hear college men sing is one of my favorite recruiting techniques. It takes some considerable effort on the director's part, but it is worth it to find a quality men's chorus in your area and either take your choir into its space or invite the chorus onto your campus. Plan a joint concert where both choirs sing individually and then come together for a combined number or two. Your students want to work with other conductors, but they will also want to see you conduct the visiting group. While the musical experience is always the most important aspect of such an endeavor, the camaraderie among performers is an invaluable tool in recruiting for your program.

Movement. Choreography, for some, is a huge nuisance. For others, riser choreography is crucial and loved by both singer and audience member alike. Boys will not mind dancing provided the movements are boy-appropriate. Silly choreography will quickly become a joke and turn pointless. The challenge becomes finding movements well-suited to your male singers. One remedy is to engage and involve the singers when creating the dance moves. If they create it, they'll dance it. It's that simple.

The other, less budget-conscious method is to hire a skilled instructor who possesses an understanding of the style and age group. Before adding movement, be sure the piece calls for it. Sometimes the most effective choreography is none at all.

For example, my first teaching position was in a school where the varsity mixed show choir ruled the choral program. Not being raised in this tradition, my goal was to find interesting ways of combining my love of classical repertoire with that of the lighter show-choir literature. As such, I programmed a set of spirituals arranged by William Dawson and Moses Hogan. Unaccompanied, the thirty students performed *Ain't That Good News* (available TTBB a cappella, arr. William Dawson, Neil A. Kjos Music Co.) standing on black boxes holding laminated newspapers. Close, flip, turn, turn, turn, pass to the right, bodies left, heads up, papers down, etc. It was high-energy, up-tempo, "legit" choral repertoire in a show-choir setting staged as best I knew how. The ballad that followed, Hogan's *I Stood on the River of Jordan*, was much easier to stage. For this number, singers moved their stage props aside and gathered downstage, center. Some sat while others kneeled or stood. No movement. Stillness. It was effective for creating a contrasting sound and mood.

For a men's chorus, his *Rise an' Shine* (TTBB div. a cappella, Hal Leonard) would provide plenty of teachable moments and would be a wonderful contrast to the opening number.

Perhaps a less erudite way of being "cool" is to incorporate props and costumes into your performance. There are many options here, but it's no surprise boys can enjoy dressing up as girls from time to time. This is especially true if the boys are doing so FOR the girls! Cheerleaders and 1980s pop stars are just a few ideas that have seen success by many men's chorus conductors.

The name game. Give your ensemble a good name and do not be afraid to change the name when the need arises. While some traditions cannot be broken, and I dare not suggest conductors try to break long-held traditions, many such things are no more than habit and carry no valid tether. The famous saying "We have always done it that way" doesn't make it the best way to do it!

For three years, I taught at University School, an all-boys independent college preparatory school outside of Cleveland, Ohio. The mascot of the school is named "Prescott, the Prepper" and resembles the Bob's Big Boy figurine. When I arrived at "US," there were two ensembles: Glee Club and US Males, a twelve-member a cappella ensemble modeled after collegiate a cappella. US Males is an obvious pun, but when it came time to establish a freshmen-only choir, it took a school-wide contest to come up with a suitable name. "Prepper Chorus" was the clear winner, as it referenced both the mascot and the preparatory nature of this ensemble.

The signature song. Many if not most collegiate choirs sing school spirit songs to end every concert. Such songs include the fight song and the alma mater. There are also instances of college glee clubs that sing a standard piece of the male chorus repertoire to open or close each performance. These become "signature tunes" the audience expects and looks forward to hearing. For example, many choirs open every concert with the piece for which this book is named, Edward Elgar's *Brothers, Sing On* arranged by Howard McKinney (Alfred Publishing 96842). The Morehouse College Glee Club performs Wendall Whelum's arrangement of Via Olatunji's *Betelehemu* (Lawson-Gould Music Publishers 52647) at nearly all of its public performances. Whether you use a song unique to your program or not, creating this type of tradition is a wonderful way to build expectation and excitement for both your singers and your audience members alike.

EXPOSURE, EXPOSURE

Perform as often as possible. Limiting performances to a concert hall setting is not advised. Celebrate learning milestones with mini performances on campus. For example, you spend all week working the most challenging section of a song. The ensemble isn't perfect, but the entire song can be sung without stopping and musical nuance is beginning to take hold. It's time to "go on the road." Take your entire ensemble to a neighboring classroom and ask that teacher if your students might sing for their peers. It takes just moments and your students will love the exposure. Furthermore, the students in the other class love the interruption!

MAKE IT FUN

This is one of those statements that is nearly impossible to interpret and even harder to plan. What may be fun for one person is not so for another. What you, the conductor, find fun may not turn out to be fun for your choir members. Unfortunately, fun cannot be imposed upon anyone. Time and again, I have realized that fun is associated and comes with those things we do well. When we take pride in our accomplishments, we are able to look back upon the process and find the enjoyment in it. Naturally, success is pleasurable.

Sometimes, it is fun to look back at the challenges we shared learning a piece of music. When I was teaching high school, the final concert of the year most often consisted of lighter fare. The exception to that was the one piece of music voted upon by the students to perform again. No song we had performed during that school year was off-limits. Without fail, each and every one of my choirs picked the most challenging piece of music, almost always in a foreign language, and the piece that had given me, the director, the most heartache during the learning process. Taking pride in a musical accomplishment surpasses any ice cream social or box step combination we force upon our singers. No matter what music we choose, and how we present it, quality must be top-notch. When we program for success, fun will ensue!

I'M STARTING A MEN'S CHORUS FOR MY NINTH- AND TENTH-GRADERS. WHAT ARE THE BEST WAYS YOU HAVE FOUND TO RECRUIT NEW SINGERS?

(Kevin Meidl) Go to where the boys are! Choir directors often hide away in the music wing of a school. Recruiting requires visibility on campus. Perhaps one way to be visible with boys is to coach a sports team. A choir director who is an assistant or head coach in football, basketball, baseball, or another highly visible sport is in an ideal position to recruit male students. However, I know of few music educators who feel qualified to coach at this level, so it is perhaps more likely a choral director will need to simply be seen at sporting events and make an effort to support male athletes.

Another place where the boys can be found is the lunchroom. Supervising or visiting the dining area on a daily basis is absolutely vital to recruiting both boys and girls. Many students sign up for classes just because their friends do. Even parents can be powerless to override the influence of friends when it comes to scheduling classes and extracurricular activities. The lunchroom is a place where a teacher will find many students who are not in choir and who have never wandered into the music wing. By talking to current choir members and observing various peer interactions, a choir director can recruit quickly and effectively.

By being visible and talking to parents, a director will allow boys to be more aware of the opportunity to sing in choir. Make the choir special and important to the entire school. Give your choir a clever name and have it perform a halftime show in the gym. Be sure to have great outfits and perform the best music that fits the ensemble. Also, make posters with memorable logos to hang throughout the school and community. In short, make it THE THING to do and a MUST-HAVE experience for boys.

(Christine Bass) Ask your present singers, especially the girls, to recommend their friends. I use a "Quality Guy" sign-up sheet where they write the name of the student, but also the singers bring their friends in to meet me and sing for me. The choral student who brings in the most guys wins an iTunes card. I am not ashamed to beg, borrow, and steal to get more guys involved in choir!

GLEE CLUB IS POPULAR WITH MY FRESHMEN AND SOPHOMORES, BUT THE OLDER STUDENTS HAVE MOVED ON TO OTHER ELECTIVES. WHAT SHOULD I DO? WHAT'S WORKED FOR YOU?

(Kerry Brennan) Teenagers are influenced by incentives. While a chorus is one of the last great democratic art forms, there can be distinctions made as a result of seniority. Who are the section leaders? Who are the officers? Who is eligible for solos? At two different schools, I have instituted a Senior Concert, the final concert of the year, in which graduating seniors are featured and honored, given tokens of their association and commitment, and celebrated as leaders of an organization marked by excellence, tradition, and camaraderie. I also instituted in both places—Roxbury Latin in Boston and University School in Cleveland—traditions of annual touring. Most years this involved a one-week domestic tour over spring break marked by concerts, church service music, occasional collaborations, tourist excursions, and fun. Every few years the tour would take us to Europe, a special treat worth aiming toward musically and worth sticking around to participate in.

At both schools I also insisted that no one was left behind because his family could not afford the trip, and financial aid was readily and generously available. Often the possibility of making an even more selective, hipper ensemble drawn from within the larger chorus (an a cappella group) keeps boys around—as they long for that even greater adulation and more challenging, more contemporary repertoire.

Finally, in "competing" with other electives, ensure there is a level playing field in regard to credit and grading, and especially ensure that the distinctive benefits—the challenge, the teamwork, the joy of artistic collaboration, the satisfaction of delighting an audience, the exposure to a potential life-long pursuit—are well-known. I have been successful in two schools in guaranteeing that Glee Club is never scheduled against another "singleton" course; in other words, there are no conflicts. Of course the best ways to keep boys involved are keeping the process interesting and fun, attending assiduously to selections of repertoire, ensuring a variety of rehearsal techniques, and planning energizing collaborations and joint concerts. It helps if the director is musically demanding, excellent, balanced, articulate, charismatic, fun, and delighted by the company of his/her singers.

HOW DO I ACTUALLY ASK STUDENTS TO SING IN MY PROGRAM? WHAT DO I SAY?

(Ethan Sperry) The problem many of us have in recruiting is that we are desperate for more male singers, and that comes across in the way we ask people to join. The singers think we need them and that gives them all the power. How many choirs have their best tenors missing lots of rehearsals because they know the conductor cannot afford to get rid of them?

The truth is that singing in choir changes people's lives for the better, usually vastly for the better. Everyone reading this book knows this to be true. When we recruit singers, we have something so valuable to offer them. You'd be amazed at how differently a person responds to an "ask" depending on the attitude of the person asking. It's important to convey your conviction that you are asking these men to join your choir for their own benefit, not just yours. Then, we need to ask everyone in sight.

Some people would rather be approached by an instructor to join the ensemble, while others would rather it be by a peer. Some need even more coaxing. I involve all my returning singers in the recruiting process. They know how much choir means to them and they want to have their friends (and even strangers) experience it as well. The students who do the best recruiting are often the ones who were "suckered" into being in choir in the first place; they are able to articulate how their initial ambivalence about choir turned into real conviction.

I have story after story of guys who joined choir because:

- A cute girl asked him.

- He saw that the choir was going on tour and he wanted to go too.

- His best friend wouldn't stop annoying him until he auditioned.

- The information session had free candy bars.

- The teacher asked and seemed genuinely interested in having him in choir.

And these are all stories of guys who have told me that choir was their *favorite* activity in high school or college. People who may have initially had no intention of joining choir, and are subsequently so glad they did, will always be your best recruiters.

(Jefferson Johnson) I find the best recruiters at the University of Kentucky are the students themselves. We empower them to be proactive in bringing new singers to our group. To that goal, I have offered various rewards for the singer who brings in the most new members in a semester. Whatever it takes! Also, our choir president annually sends a letter to targeted high schools asking for contact info for their male singers. He then follows up with a personal letter to each prospective singer with more information on our program.

(Christine Bass) Many who sang before have now stopped and those are the ones to recruit. Ask your feeder school to give you a list of everyone who sang at all in middle school. Reference lists from elementary and junior high choirs/honors choirs. Contact those guys and say, "Hey, I heard you sang before. How about trying the high school choir?"

(Kevin Meidl) Many students will sign up for choir if they are asked directly by you—the choir teacher. Guidance counselors often call students into their offices for scheduling and to make general suggestions for course registration. Students can be blindly led into classes they neither want nor need. Meeting potential singers in the lunchroom and asking them to sign up for choir offers clear direction for the student when guidance appointment day arrives. The most powerful things a teacher can do are 1) invite the child to sing in choir; 2) give him a letter of acceptance into choir to present to his guidance counselor; and 3) follow up with an email to the guidance counselor and parents expressing how excited you are to have him in your choir. Recruiting is a one-on-one, very personal experience between a teacher and student.

Ask your students for help, too! New freshmen and even sophomores in high school are virtually unknown to a choir director. Yet, these kids have been in school for many years with each other and have attended general music and choir classes together in the past. Current singers in a choir will always know other good singers in school who should be participating but for one reason or another have left the program. They can be recruited back! Enlist student help. Ask them to generate a list of past singers whom you can contact. Then, have your current students bring prospective singers to the choir room to meet you in a comfortable setting outside of actual class time.

SHOULD I USE REPERTOIRE TO RECRUIT SINGERS TO MY PROGRAM? DO YOU HAVE PIECES YOU GO TO WHEN IT'S TIME TO RECRUIT? IF SO, WHAT ARE THEY?

(Gary Schwartzhoff) I believe repertoire is the textbook for the academic course—the choral ensemble. I select repertoire on the basis of the needs of the ensemble and the annual need to expose the ensemble to music from all historical periods. I have not selected repertoire specifically to fulfill the purpose of recruitment, yet given the nature of the ensemble, there are works that appear annually in our repertoire, including the traditional school spirit songs, *I Have Had Singing* by Ron Jeffers, and a choral benediction. These works become the core repertoire that the ensemble uses to develop good choral technique and brotherhood within the ensemble.

(Kevin Meidl) When recruiting or building a new male chorus, it is important to understand the dynamic of programming. Begin programming with repertoire that immediately grabs the attention of the singers and is exciting for the audience. This does not necessarily mean a "pop" concert, but rather a program that can be musically successful and will encourage the boys to show off their new choir. Themes such as Barbershop, Multicultural/ World Music, Boys on Broadway, Real Men Sing, Songs of the Sea, Boy Bands of the '60s, or South of the Border Fiesta! can all be winning programs that will help recruit boys to your program. The choice of excellent, quality repertoire is critical regardless of genre. In addition, the successful preparation of the choir from musical, logistical, and presentation (lights, sound, props, movement, staging) standpoints will build pride and excitement that will help in the recruiting effort.

(Frank Bianchi) I use a quartet of older singers to perform for school functions, such as singing the National Anthem at school athletic events.

WHAT ARE SOME TANGIBLE RECRUITING TOOLS I CAN USE?

(Jefferson Johnson) We host an event called "Male Chorus Day." One Saturday in January, male singers (eighth through twelfth grade) come to campus for a day of rehearsing three TTBB pieces. I conduct the rehearsals and a performance at the end of the day, but a powerful component is an hour-long clinic with the sixteen-man a cappella group the acoUstiKats. The high school singers split into their four voice parts and have a clinic with the acoUstiKats on their respective parts. During this time, the "Kats" teach an entire pop song to the young singers. This peer teaching is mutually beneficial to everyone and is a big draw for our event. The concert at the end of the day is informal and features a selected high school all-male ensemble, the UK Men's Chorus, a set by the acoUstiKats, the entire high school group with the acoUstiKats on the newly learned pop piece, and the three pieces the large group of singers learned that day.

(Thomas Jenrette)

1. Host a male choral festival.

    Plan a night of male choral music and invite choral directors to join your ensemble in a concert conducted by you. Invite choral directors to bring as many students as they wish, but be aware that some singers will come with the music memorized, while some will come having never seen it before. Pick repertoire you can assemble with minimal rehearsal time. If possible, visit each school from which the singers are coming to help them prepare ahead of time. Allowing singers to become acquainted with you and your teaching style in a more intimate setting can be the best thing you can do to recruit singers. Also, this type of choral event provides an opportunity for young male singers to sing in a larger, hopefully more mature and experienced male choral ensemble. This should be a thrilling, new musical experience for everyone. I believe most males prefer singing in a good all-male ensemble to a mixed choir, but unfortunately, they may not have had the opportunity to experience all-male choral singing. By providing this experience, you can introduce young men to an activity they will want to continue...and with you!

2. Send your students into the schools.

    Pick a day that will be convenient for those choral directors whose students you wish to recruit, and ask them if some of your male singers might visit their rehearsal to work with their male singers. Your singers should do whatever the school director would like to assist in the rehearsal, such as work on vocal exercises, teach parts, or just participate in the rehearsal as ensemble singers. Hopefully, the school director will permit your students to talk about their experiences in your ensemble and how much it means to them. If you have forty singers in your male ensemble, you might send four singers to each of ten schools on the same day. Be sure to have your students take along cards for the prospective students to fill out so that you can follow up with a personal communication.

3. Visit rehearsals of other ensembles.

    Similar to the idea listed above, contact choral directors whose students you wish to recruit, and offer your own services. Volunteer for whatever the director would like you to do—warm up, talk about vocal technique, or conduct the rehearsal. If the ensemble you are visiting is a mixed ensemble, offer to work with the men separately while the choral director works with the women. This not only gives the students the opportunity to get to know you, but it gives you the opportunity to find out which singers you would like to recruit.

CHAPTER 12
FUND-RAISING

As any music director, choral or otherwise, surely knows, raising money is not only a challenge to do, but it is also tedious and often frustrating as well. Fund-raising events are most often nonmusical in nature and take time away from rehearsal and score study. They become a nuisance for those who choose to participate and frequently yield less money than expected and needed. Cookie dough, car-wash detergent, Easter lilies, and pumpkins have all served nonprofits well over time and money is certainly raised from these endeavors, but few help us reach the musical goals we set forth at the outset of our season. Furthermore, these nonmusical fund-raisers impart little on the chorus's overall camaraderie and the ensemble's ability to sing.

The goal of fund-raising is just that—to raise funds to pay for programming, curricular and extracurricular, that is not being financed otherwise. In a world where funding for the arts is cut year after year, music programs (and those who administer them) are forced to find ways of paying for sheet music, uniforms, props, entry fees, instrument repair and rental, and travel to and from contests and tour venues. Many school districts simply do not allocate monies to "extracurricular" activities such as the performing and creative arts. As choral directors and teachers who recognize the unrivaled value of the programs we offer, we find ourselves willing to take on the tedious task of fund-raising—again and again and again.

Peddling candy, Christmas tree ornaments, and T-shirts are all acceptable and common methods of fund-raising, yet, as mentioned, none of these campaigns relates to the music we make or the team we hope to build. Why, then, do we subject ourselves and our performers to these daunting, tedious, and, quite frankly, embarrassing requests? What boy enjoys selling vanilla-scented wax candles to Grandma and Grandpa? What nineteen-year-old glee club member wants to walk into a sorority house and ask, "Who wants to buy a book of discount coupons?" Furthermore, for every candle or six-pack of popcorn sold, the singer often makes just 40 percent of the sale, leaving 60 percent—the majority of the profit—to the manufacturer!

This brand of fund-raising is common and has certainly been proved successful to some degree, but it bears no educational value for our music education, our programming, or the success of our singers. With this in mind, I offer several music-based ideas, albeit sometimes loosely related, that offer performance and team-building opportunities. Remember, as conductors and educators it is our duty to find and implement those programs with "teachable moments" whenever possible.

SING-ATHON

A "typical" sing-athon or rehearsal-athon is measured by the total length of time that continuous singing takes place. Do not assume this is full *tutti* choir rehearsal, but rather choral work being done. While one section rehearses or performs, others are playing volleyball, face-painting, or having "nap time." This practical and useful fund-raiser is successful provided there is plenty of supervision and nonsinging activities are well-planned and coordinated.

Do not be afraid, however, to create a fund-raiser where rehearsal time is rewarded. For example, for every hour of rehearsal preparing for a concert, donors pledge a mere ten cents. Twelve weeks of rehearsal with four rehearsals per week equals forty-eight rehearsals. With each student collecting $4.80 from ten sponsors—not a big ask—that's a total of $48 from each student. Multiply that by fifty singers and you've raised $2,400 toward your goal. Imagine doing this during each concert period for a total of four mini fund-raisers and voilà! Your program just raised nearly $10,000!

MADRI"GUY" DINNER

Modeled after the "Madrigal Dinner" or "Madrigal Feast," this event is nearly identical to many popular forms of dinner theater. Most often, the dinner is set in the Middle Ages and involves a comic plot complete with costumes and props. The plot, of sorts, typically connects the courses and is followed by a more formal concert. Often, a traditional song or carol precedes each food course as well.

Tickets are sold for the dinner by singers and the meal is often potluck. If held at a school, the overhead is generally minimal.

Programming comedic repertoire, such as *Manly Men* (Kurt Knecht, Walton Music WJMS1031), or a Renaissance carol, such as the Spanish villancico *Riu, Riu Chiu* (arr. Jim Leininger, Alliance Music Publishing AMP0383), makes for a truly entertaining evening with musical merit and plenty of "teachable choral moments" for your ensemble and audience.

Madri"guy" dinners are effective and appropriate any time of year and work especially well at the holidays, at Valentine's Day, or as a "Spring Fling" event.

Tree Lightings

Most communities have tree lighting festivities in late November or early December. Bring a small ensemble to sing carols or selections from your holiday concert repertoire. This public and free offering allows your singers to promote their concert and offers yet another performance opportunity. Set up a table with concert ticket information as well as a donation jar. Some members may decide to "pass the hat" at the conclusion of the event. A brief announcement introducing the ensemble, along with a personal plea for support during this time of giving, goes a long way with community members. As it is typical for choruses to include singers of many religious (or nonreligious) backgrounds, be sensitive to those who don't celebrate Christmas.

Tailgating with merchandise sales

Many university glee clubs have mastered Saturday morning, pre-football-game tailgating as a suitable and fun fund-raising activity. During my own time at the University of Michigan, these were called "Record Sings." A dozen or more guys would don festive school attire and meet several hours before the big game. Some glee clubs choose do this activity wearing formal concert wear rather than their school colors. At the assigned gathering place several hours before kickoff, each singer is given merchandise items to hold on to—CDs, T-shirts, sweatshirts. The group then meanders throughout the various lawns and parking lots, offering a verse or two of a school song to each group of tailgaters. At the conclusion of the song, singers walk through the crowd offering the CDs and T-shirts and accepting donations from those not interested in purchasing something. A dollar here and a dollar there certainly will add up to a nice pot at the end of the day!

It is imperative that a speaker is nominated from within your traveling ensemble to announce who you are and how the donations will be used. For example: "Hi. We're from the University of Michigan Men's Glee Club. We're raising money for our fall retreat and we'd like to sing a little something for you. We hope you enjoy!" By making this a statement rather than a question, your audience has no opportunity to say, "No, thank you." They then feel compelled to listen and hopefully will offer a monetary tip. Be sure to have those donation buckets available. This idea works well on football Saturday, but it can be done at citywide festivals, at a community pool, outside the grocery store on a Saturday morning, or before any event attracting large groups of people.

ADOPT-A-SINGER

Get out those puppy-dog eyes and pouty lips because you'll need them for this fund-raising activity! The adopt-a-singer program is just that—an opportunity for family members, friends and community supporters to directly help your program. It works this way: Your glee club is going to New York City to perform at Carnegie Hall. The mantra for your adopt-a-singer program might read:

SINGABLE
LOVEABLE
ADOPTABLE

It is most definitely a cheesy mantra and many readers will groan upon reading it, but the concept is good and it works.

The adopt-a-singer idea is an honest approach to fund-raising. There are no gimmicks, nothing to buy, and no catalogues to peruse. Instead, the singer explains the benefits of the undertaking—choir tour, CD recording, contest admission fee, and/or uniform expense—and asks for outright financial support.

This fund-raiser works well as a 50/50 too. Fifty percent of the donated income goes directly into the singer's account, while 50 percent goes to the general operating fund or a fund designated by the chorus's administration. For the recipient of the adopt-a-singer money, this program is a lesson in communal investment as well as in individual support. For the donor, supporting the greater cause, as well as the individual, is usually a great selling point.

A few words of caution about this program: Donors should not be asked to make cash contributions and checks should not be made out to individual singers. All monies should go through proper, official channels, such as the school music department or club office. Be sure to recognize those who've given to your program in your concert program or annual handout. Thank-you letters are a MUST for every donation!

SINGERS GIVE BACK: BUILDING COMMUNITY

Camaraderie among singers outside the choir room is just as important as it is inside. "Singers Give Back" is an idea based on the premise of mission work.

Imagine a scenario such as this: The total music budget was slashed at the start of the school year. In years past, both the varsity men's choir and the freshmen men's choir participated in the statewide all-male honor choir. It's held not far from the state capitol building and a renowned clinician is always hired to conduct. Your freshmen get the chance to sing with hundreds of other high school boys; the educational impact is immeasurable.

The cost of the trip is approximately $100 per student, which covers transportation, meals, registration, and music. Because of the reduced budget, your freshmen men's choir is now unable to attend.

"Singers Give Back" can help. One method is to create teams—three boys with one adult supervisor. Each team is charged with earning $300 by means of paid community service. A few ideas of how to do this:

- Offer neighbors the following service: spring garden clean-up, complete with flowerbeds raked, gardens weeded, driveways and walkways swept, and all refuse bagged for curbside disposal. $50 per household. Three boys—three hours of time.

- Snow day! Walk the neighborhoods offering snow-clearing assistance. Three boys can shovel a lot of snow in a short period of time. If one has a snow blower, the other two can de-ice or sweep off walkways. $25 per driveway. Three boys—twenty-five minutes of time.

- Many states have bottle and can redemption programs. While most states offer five cents per returned bottle, some offer ten cents. If you think this won't add up to much, I know from personal experience that an afternoon picking up soda cans in the local park quickly earns you $10, $20, $30, and even more when you do so after a town-wide fair. When I was in junior high school, quite some time ago, I collected more than a thousand cans in one afternoon!

- Do the odd job for those who detest odd jobs. We all have jobs around the house that get put off year after year. These range from vacuuming the basement to sweeping out the garage and cleaning gutters. Three high school boys—three hours. $100.

Advertise this fundraiser around neighborhoods, community centers, office buildings, and the town square. Provide students with fliers they can distribute, at church and synagogue, at their parents' workplaces, and to visitors at soccer games. You'll be surprised how many people will support the efforts of students appreciating the value of a dollar. For example:

High School Music Department Sponsors

SINGERS GIVE BACK!
A Freshmen Men's Choir Fund-Raiser

We Clean. We Sweep.
We Garden. We Plant.
We Move. We Shovel.

AND
WE SING.

*Three high school boys
do the heavy work for you.*
All donations help us go to State Honor Choir Festival.

**Call ninth-grader Noah Weston at 555-1234
to schedule your service.**

RAFFLES

Be sure to abide by the lottery laws in your area, but raffles can be huge moneymakers if done correctly. In order to provide "teachable moments" relating to music, many find success using the "Conduct the Chorus" raffle. Winners receive a one-on-one conducting lesson with you, the trained conductor, and a guest spot on your concert. Prepare your singers for this musical event by changing the tempo of the work from rehearsal to rehearsal and mixing up your gestures; for example, missing the downward gesture on beat one or using no conducting pattern at all. Learning to follow various conductors' styles is definitely something to be taught and learned.

Other raffle winnings might include a private performance by an ensemble at a house party or spring barbeque, a framed octavo signed by every member of the choir, or perhaps an opportunity to narrate a concert or portion of a concert. Multiple prize packages are also highly desired. For example: dinner for two at a local restaurant (donated, of course), reserved seating at the performance, and a private toast in the conductor's dressing room after the concert. The key to raffles is to make the prize coveted and unique.

POPS CONCERTS

(Kevin Meidl) Pops concerts may be the most immediately successful fund-raising events for choral programs. These can be programs featuring various choirs and combined ensembles, or student-organized ensembles that are auditioned for the final program. In either case, tickets can be marketed for pops concerts at a higher price per seat because of the nature of the event or if it is billed as a fund-raiser. Annual pops concerts become huge moneymakers for school music programs.

Although pops concerts are common across the country, other popular genres that have the same successful result include cabaret, barbershop, holiday classics, madrigal dinners, and Broadway reviews. As fund-raising concerts become tradition, choral programs can begin to build libraries of music, costumes, and prop collections that can be reused in future years. These archives reduce expenses and improve revenue for music departments.

SINGING VALENTINES

(Kevin Meidl) Arguably, the best-known and most popular fund-raiser among all-male ensembles is the Singing Valentine program. Many schools have barbershop quartets or small ensembles that go out to private homes or businesses around Valentine's Day. Some schools have all-male ensembles that are available year-round to serenade at birthdays, anniversaries, and private events. Revenue can be continuously generated!

RECORDINGS

(Kevin Meidl) Recording technology is widely available and easy to use. Where only a decade ago sophisticated recording engineers would be required to produce a high-quality CD or DVD, today many students own and have experience making their own recordings. Themed CDs, such as pops or Christmas, have the potential to sell very well. In addition, sampler CDs with more than one choir on the label allow more students to be invested in the fund-raising program and the creation of the CD itself.

The recording process can be very educational and rewarding for both conductor and choir member alike. Dedicating rehearsal time to achieve the highest quality results along with playback review of recorded tracks can be informative and very positive for the growth of a choir. Students involved with musical decisions become more engaged in the recording process and more invested in the final product. This investment manifests itself later in greater sales of the recording. A secondary result of a recording sale is the positive promotion of the men's choir or program throughout the community.

CHAPTER 13
TRAVEL

It is said that travel is the only thing you buy that makes you richer.

Whether I am taking part as a performer, conductor, or group leader, going on a tour is one of the things I most enjoy doing.

Picture it: 1992. I was a member of the Greater Boston Youth Symphony Orchestra percussion section. We set up an impromptu jam session in Prague's Old Town Square and dragged out every instrument we had brought over from the States. For some reason, I chose to play a pair of congas and a large, beat-up cowbell. We drummed for several hours and collected quite a few Czech *korunas* (crowns). It was an amazing afternoon and I will remember it forever.

Picture it: 1996. I was on tour with the University of Michigan Men's Glee Club and we were in Buenos Aires, Argentina. My host family allowed me to use their car for the evening provided I take along their two teenage kids. Of course! My host brother and sister led us all over the city pointing out major sights and showing us true Argentinian nightlife. We were just a block away from home when...BOOM! I drove us right into a pothole. No, it was more akin to a sinkhole. With a flat tire and a dented wheel rim, I drove the car home, albeit at a snail's pace.

"Oh, you fell in!" said my host dad.

"I am SO sorry! It was dark and..."

He raised his hand, as if to toast my accident, and said in his severely broken English, "Everything okay. I do it too this week. Now we get new tire. Shiny one. *Salud!*"

Everyone laughed—I nervously so.

Picture it: March 22, 2003. I'm with the University School Glee Club in Stockholm, Sweden, on the last leg of our ten-day Scandinavian tour and I've corralled all fifty high school boys into a hotel conference room. "Gentlemen," I said, "about an hour ago, our U.S. military began an attack on Baghdad. I want us to stay together for the time being, but I will turn on the television so we can all watch the news. Everyone should call home tonight to check in with your parents."

That military mission became known as the night of Shock and Awe.

University School Glee Club 2003 tour to Sweden
Noel banquet site, Stockholm City Hall

Picture it: July 2010. It's nearing 100 degrees inside the massive stone church and there is no air circulating whatsoever. The Turtle Creek Chorale is performing in the heart of Barcelona's Gothic Quarter. It's standing room only behind the pews and I'm conducting Biebl's beloved setting of the *Ave Maria* text. Every singer is soaked with sweat, but focused solely on the performance. Just as we begin to sing the tender amens at the end of the piece, a lone church bell, high above, begins to ring the hour. Perfectly in tune, the bell accompanied us through the final cadence. Magical, memorable, and thankfully caught on video.

Going on tour should be thrilling and exotic, but also educational and valuable. It is, though, usually a stressful and daunting task for the conductor. It is my experience on tour that the conductor is asked to make nearly every decision that impacts the ensemble as a whole. For example, what time is the wake-up call? Seems like a simple question, but do you want them at breakfast early, or was it a late night and do you prefer they sleep in just a little? How long will it take for your men to get up and moving? Will bodies be warmed up if you allow just an hour's time? Perhaps it's Sunday and the concert is at 5 p.m. What time should meals be scheduled for that day? Should we have a late lunch and late dinner, or lunch at the normal time with a small snack before the concert? Decisions like these, in my experience, become the conductor's to make.

Decisions directly affecting musical performance are not the only ones referred to the conductor while on the road. A conductor's responsibility significantly broadens to include tour director, parent, minister, and even scapegoat when this need arises. Referring to the Iraq war anecdote previously mentioned, I'll never forget one twelfth-grader who asked to see me in private after watching the bombing on television. This young man was not only the president of the glee club, he was also one of the most developed—mentally and physically—of the bunch. The boy had just seen war for the first time, and truth be told, so had I. The door to the conference room closed and I don't think this boy got out two words before he broke down sobbing. Terrified, he wanted to go home. He cried for a few moments and I reassured him of his own safety and well-being. Simply put, he needed a hug. For a teacher, however, hugging a student is viewed as an inappropriate act. In this moment, it became my job to act as parent more than as conductor or teacher. With the student calmed down, together we called his parents. This experience has certainly stayed with me over the years and I would imagine has stayed with him too.

Dramatic experiences aside, traveling with a chorus will undoubtedly provide many of the most rewarding experiences of one's musical career. Planning and executing a successful tour requires great knowledge, organization, creativity, and a lot of research. Furthermore, all of this comes with the great expense of time. Hiring a professional tour company alleviates much of the stress, but it often comes at a price. So as not to get ahead of myself, let's approach this topic in a strategic fashion.

Photo Credit: Michael McGary

Turtle Creek Choral 2010 tour to Spain
Verano de la Villa Festival Royal Palace, Madrid

So you want to take your men's choir on tour? That's FANTASTIC! Ask yourself, as conductor, how many singers will adequately represent the sound of the ensemble. Not every singer will participate and that's just how it goes. No matter how much fund-raising and championing you do for the tour, not everyone will partake. As conductor of the Turtle Creek Chorale leading a ten-day trip to Spain, I knew we would not have all two hundred men travel. Would forty singers embody the sound of the Turtle Creek Chorale? Would seventy-five? Maybe the magic number of singers is 150? Whatever the case may be, it is ultimately up to the conductor to determine this expectation and desire.

Many tour leaders do not place the same weight on musical performance as they do on the travel experience itself—the *gestalt* of touring. Sometimes musical performance simply provides the motivation to travel and becomes the common connection between travelers. In this case, it may not be necessary to set a minimum or maximum number of tour participants.

To illustrate tour planning, imagine that twenty-two university-age glee clubbers have signed up to travel and that you have determined the trip will cost somewhere in the vicinity of $2,500 per paying traveler. It is time to begin campaigning for your tour destination. Choir members will most definitely have an idea of where they'd like to go, so ask them for input. Obtaining feedback from those traveling is a valuable method of increasing the overall support for the tour destination once one has been decided upon. If need be, have singers vote or rank their top three location choices.

Here's an example of how this works and why it's effective. Singers submit the following tour ideas:

China
Holland
South Africa
France
Canada and Alaska (combined as one tour)

With a budget of $2,500 per paying passenger, you automatically scratch China and South Africa off the list, knowing airfares alone may be prohibitive. This leaves potential tours to Holland or France or a Canada/Alaska adventure. You put this to a vote and the singers eliminate the North America trip, as it doesn't seem exotic enough. As conductor, you feel differently, but the goal is to have your singers excited at the outset of the planning process. This leaves Holland and France on the list. Both countries offer quality performance venues and audiences are known to be welcoming and supportive of visiting choirs. Perhaps it's time to impart your own ideas on each trip.

Here's what you might tell your chorus about France: Paris has amazing churches in which you can perform, a rich and interesting history, impressive architecture throughout the city, and many of the world's best and most famous art museums. It is easy to travel throughout France using its rail system. While the group may begin touring in Paris, you could visit Versailles before heading south to the wine region of Avignon and Aix-en-Provence, singing in glorious, ornate churches along the way. Then, everyone could spend an afternoon in Cannes, home of the renowned film festival, before finally ending the tour along the Mediterranean Sea in the French Riviera city of Nice. Furthermore, it's only an hour's train ride to Monaco, home of the world-famous Monte Carlo Casino. This trip, realistically, can be designed to stay within the approved budget.

With regard to Holland, most think of Amsterdam as being the foremost stop on this tour. A trip to the Red Light District is a must for those inclined (and allowed), but a stroll along the city's canal system is most impressive. A boat ride, a visit to the home of Anne Frank, and a performance at the Concertgebouw or inside the magnificent Rijksmuseum are just the beginning of what's possible in this fabulous, walkable city.

Beyond Amsterdam, perhaps you'll take a trip to the administrative capital city of The Hague or architecturally interesting Rotterdam. You might entice your choir to choose this itinerary by adding a visit to Belgium. Brussels, Bruges, and the extraordinary city of Antwerp are just a few hours away by bus or by train. Again, this trip can be designed to stay within your proposed budget.

You may decide to present your own suggested tour itinerary for a second vote or, if you are employing a tour company, you may ask one of its staff members to make a presentation to your ensemble. Bear in mind that the options presented should reflect the age group with whom you will travel. Amsterdam's Red Light District and France's wine country serve little purpose for high school choirs.

After much dialogue, you've done it. Voilà! Together, weighing all the options, it is decided the group will travel to France on this imaginary tour. Coordinating all aspects of such a journey is a massive responsibility, and those who do so for themselves are to be commended for their initiative. If you prefer to use a professional tour company, it's important to know what questions to ask when securing bids. A quick Internet search will provide contact information for scores of agencies vying for your business. Consider the following when comparing companies and tour bids.

University School Glee Club 2003 tour to Denmark
Copenhagen

HOW MANY ARE TRAVELING WITH YOUR GROUP?

Most often, tour companies specializing in performing groups do not offer discounted rates based on the number of singers traveling. Instead, there is a ratio of free spot to paying passenger that is written into the contract. For example, a 1:10 ratio is quite common, as is 1:20. This translates into one free spot for every ten or twenty full-fare travelers. Note: Free spots are not really free. The cost is equally divided among paying travelers. A director's free trip costing $2,500 is split twenty ways (using the 1:20 ratio). As such, an additional $125 is charged to each of your choristers. I should mention that most tour companies negotiate with group leaders on this subject. In the case where you have 100 singers traveling, you may earn five free spots. However, you may require only three free spots, for the director, accompanist, and school administrator. In this instance, many tour companies will reduce the tour cost across the board to reflect this difference. Again, ask your tour company to negotiate these prices.

HOW LONG SHOULD A CONCERT TOUR LAST?

Tour length, or number of nights away from home, is often determined by the total budget and the tour destination. About $2,500 for a weeklong tour is reasonable, keeping in mind fluctuation in airfare, fuel surcharges, and varying world economies. One must also consider the costs that eat into the bottom line, such as round-trip airfare through one airport versus multi-city airfares. Traveling over winter or spring break can severely impact not only the airfare, but also the cost of hotels, ground transportation and, in some cases, entrance fees to tourist attractions. For student groups, a school vacation period, such as spring break, is often the best time for a choir to take its tour, but tour costs may be slightly higher because so many people travel at that time.

Directors and group leaders should also consider the age of those traveling. University glee clubs are known to take much longer tours than those undertaken by high school and community ensembles. For example, I traveled with the University of Michigan on a whopping twenty-six-day tour of South America. We departed soon after the second semester final exam period and visited five countries. Multiple flights were included in the tour fee, which was significantly more than $2,500. This is certainly not the norm for most choruses, but the possibilities are endless.

WHAT SORTS OF VENUES ARE BEST FOR TOUR PERFORMANCES?

When I travel with my men, I like to provide a variety of acoustical spaces in which to sing. On one tour with the Turtle Creek Chorale, we performed in Madrid's Verano de la Villa—an outdoor music venue next to the Royal Palace. The acoustic wasn't ideal, but the experience of performing under the stars with, literally, a palatial background made for a hugely memorable and meaningful concert.

Turtle Creek Choral 2010 tour to Spain
Madrid

The second venue on our tour of Spain was a cultural center in the heart of Seville. The venue was not unlike an American concert hall, complete with plush seating, a terraced balcony, and beautifully stained hardwood stage flooring. We did, however, learn on this stop that southern Spain is akin to Florida in the summertime—snowbirds fly north and cultural activities are few and far between and are generally not well-attended. Our energy and singing were strong, but we numbered more than our audience.

The third and final performance of our trip took place in Barcelona's Santa Maria del Pi, a fourteenth-century Gothic church in the Barri Gòtic district of the city. The church's sanctuary was monumental in both size and beauty, but as is the case inside many large stone churches with vaulted ceilings, the echo from wall to wall measured nearly seven seconds! Such an acoustic required that adjustments be made to performance tempi, piano dampening and volume, and diction quality, among other things. This venue posed many challenges, but all of them were surmountable.

Collaborations with local choirs prove both educationally valuable and enjoyable for performers. Whether you are working with a travel company or arranging your own tour, it is not difficult to locate a conductor and ensemble willing to share a concert with a visiting choir. Once the connection has been made, be sure to agree upon a piece that both groups can sing together as one massed choir.

I fondly remember traveling to Puerto Rico with the Temple University Concert Choir. Our musical host that day was the Coro del San Juan Conservatorio de Musica, William Rivera, conductor. Each choir performed separately before combining to perform a few traditional Puerto Rican melodies. Not only are such group efforts rich musically, but lasting friendships are often formed among singers.

Not every choral collaboration has to be between similar ensembles, however. I remember making a tour of Italy with the Michigan State University Men's Glee Club. The second concert venue on our itinerary was to be a prestigious private school in the beautiful city of Verona. When we arrived at the school, the principal informed us that because of a rotating class schedule, the older students weren't on campus, so we would perform instead for the second- and third-grade classes. Additionally, she said the formal auditorium was under construction and our performance would take place in the school's gymnasium.

We entered the gym and saw a hundred or so children systematically taking their seats on the blue-cushioned gym floor. Everyone sat behind the free-throw line. The students were relatively well-behaved during the music itself, but as quickly as Dr. Jekyll turned into Mr. Hyde, the moment we finished our set the children stormed the mock stage begging for photos, autographs, handshakes, high fives, and hugs. In the eyes of these Italian eight- and nine-year-olds, the college men from East Lansing, Michigan, were stars—mega stars! Our concert certainly did not have the musical impact we had hoped for, yet it was precisely the kind of unique travel experience that becomes a tour story told over and over again for years to come.

How do I select repertoire to bring on tour?

Refer to the chapter titled "Programming and Repertoire Selection."

What's involved in a homestay?

Homestays require considerable effort and trust on the part of the director, but also on the part of each host. Upon arrival, each traveler or group of travelers is paired off with a host family for the duration of the stay in that city. In my experience, hosts are asked to provide a bed or sleeping space for each singer, breakfasts, post-concert snacks, and transportation to and from all pickup and drop-off points. Many hosts go above and beyond, but these are the basic needs of each singer.

Be sure singers mail a thank-you note to each host family at the conclusion of the tour. Find a magazine or piece of junk mail lying around the house and record the correct spelling of the host's name, as well as the physical address and postal code. Some directors may find it useful to provide letterhead and postage too.

There are so many hotels from which to choose! Are online references reliable?

When choosing to stay in a hotel, it's important—very important—to do your own research. When possible, ask for references from other group tour leaders. In 2008, I traveled to France with a small performing group. Our last stop on the trip was in Nice, along the French Riviera. The hotel we booked had received three stars, and the online photos suggested it was more than adequate. The hotel was near the train station and had a large breakfast area. With this limited information, it seemed like a decent place for us to stay. Boy, were we wrong!

While the staff was friendly and helpful, the rooms were terribly out of date, the shower stalls were covered in mold, the banana yellow paint was chipping in every corner, the doors squeaked, hot water lasted only seconds and, as those who have been to Nice know already, a hotel near the train station is not a selling point. To get to the Promenade, the famous strolling area along the Mediterranean Sea, it's a pleasant twenty-five-minute walk in decent weather; however, on that rainy December day, I chose to hail a taxi. A word of advice: ask how much the fare will be BEFORE getting in the cab. Had I done so, I would have saved 15 euros, or nearly $30, if I had made the walk under an umbrella. Nice was not so "nice" on my wallet after all.

When you're choosing hotels, personal references by those you trust go a long way toward making your tour a success.

WHAT DO I NEED TO KNOW ABOUT CHOOSING A HOTEL?

My list could go on and on, but here are a few basic questions you should ask when choosing a hotel for group travel:

- How close is the hotel to tourist attractions? Buses are expensive. Be sure your hotel is near public transportation, such as a bus, rail, or subway station.

- How many beds are in a room? Boys will share beds, but they don't like to do it. Two double beds will sleep four comfortably; however, most boys prefer sleeping in a rollaway cot to sharing a bed. Some will even choose to sleep in a sleeping bag on the floor. Yes, a sleeping bag over a bed...

- Is breakfast included in the price? What does breakfast include and what are the hours of service?

- Is wireless Internet access available in the hotel? Is it available in each room or in the lobby only? Is there a fee to use the Internet?

- What times are check-in and check-out? This often affects tour schedules, etc.

- Is a restaurant or convenience store on site or nearby? Singers like to get snacks at odd hours of the day and night.

How do I plan for gratuities?

This is perhaps the most overlooked facet of touring. Imagine this scenario—each singer has paid his $2,500 tour cost. They have been told this sum will cover travel expenses, excursions and sightseeing, two meals per day, and all possible surcharges. You suggest they bring roughly $25 in extra spending money for each day of the tour. On a ten-day tour, they have an additional $250 or so to spend on lunches, snacks, souvenirs, etc. The last day arrives and you stand before them with your final announcements.

It's time to collect tips for the tour guide who has been with your group since you arrived, as well as for the bus driver. The tour company, if you've used one, has suggested each person tip $8 for each day of the tour. Singers open their wallets to discover they didn't budget for an extra $80. There is nothing left to give. Furthermore, they've been told all surcharges were included.

In 2011, I traveled to South Korea with a musical delegation. The tour company that coordinated this particular adventure included all gratuities in the original tour package price. On this tour, tipping was never discussed and those with empty billfolds on day eight had no reason to panic. Smart planning. Plain and simple, DO NOT FORGET TO PLAN FOR GRATUITIES!

Why do you travel with your high school ensemble and how do you choose tour destinations? How often did you travel?

(Frank Bianchi) With high school students, my intent was to build camaraderie within the group and allow students an opportunity to perform in a culturally rich and oftentimes big city. For me, it is important to offer experiences for my students they might otherwise not have at home. These include visits to the theater, concerts in world-class auditoriums, and visits to cultural centers and famous museums. Again, it was about building camaraderie. I liked to travel every two to three years with my high school ensembles.

(Jameson Marvin) Touring is a terrific way to get to know each other. Without any doubt, touring (and singing the major SATB symphonic-choral works with our women's and mixed choirs) has been consistently the greatest experience for the Harvard Glee Club. Each year, we take a one-week spring tour and every fourth summer we take a major international tour. It is truly a bonding experience. Touring and singing many concerts also becomes a natural and evolving musical experience. Most important, the Glee Club knows the music so well that we can truly make music together, instinctively. Singers become a well-oiled *ensemble* with tremendous flexibility that can achieve new nuances spontane-ously—the highest artistic level.

Sitting on a bus next to singers you have seen only in rehearsals allows for the possibility of new friendships. Sharing laughter, common and strange experiences, and remarkable stories make wonderful memories. Memories are also made when you sing a fabulous concert or go to a new and exciting location in the United States, or when visiting another country.

Michigan State University Men's Glee Club 2007 tour to Italy
Singing the alma mater in the colosseum in Rome

DO YOU PREFER HOTELS OR HOMESTAYS WHEN TRAVELING? IS FUND-RAISING INVOLVED IN THIS DECISION?

(Jameson Marvin) All extracurricular activities at Harvard receive no funding from the university. For the Glee Club, two endowments do help (to some degree) pay for transpor-tation, at least continentally. When in the States, we try to house with local college choirs or community choirs and alumni. We often share stages with other choirs, in exchange for housing. We are frequently sponsored by local organizations that offer concert series.

On tours to foreign countries, we have to raise a great deal of money. For a five-week tour, for example, to Scandinavia or South Africa or Japan/China/Hong Kong, we raise funds by asking alumni and families and from doing gigs around and near Harvard and on spring tours at high schools. All singers may go on tour, but we ask each to obtain no less than a fourth of the total tour cost if at all possible.

Tours, like all choral activities at Harvard, are student-managed. Over two-year periods, general locations are determined, then cities and venues, then housing opportunities, and then transportations costs, and then fund-raising begins. It is a remarkable process led by remarkable students. Former managers and tour managers of Harvard Glee Club are now or have been managers of the New York Philharmonic, the Chicago Symphony Chorus, the North Carolina Symphony, and so on.

DO YOU USE A TRAVEL COMPANY OR PLAN YOUR OWN TRIPS? WHY? WHAT DO I ASK WHEN RESEARCHING A TOUR COMPANY?

(Paul Rardin) I prefer to use a travel company. While I probably have the resources to locate decent venues and activities in the cities I want to visit, I do not have the time or the resources to ensure good publicity and full houses along the way. It is the job of reputable travel companies to publicize smartly and heavily and I always find it to be worth the extra money to have this done professionally.

I ask travel companies the following questions prior to signing contracts:

- How long have you been in business?

- What percentage of your clients are choral ensembles?

- How many tours have you organized for the cities/regions we are hoping to visit?

- Will you give me names and contact information of the conductors of these tours or of the last three choral tours? May I contact them about your work?

- Who are your musical contacts in the cities/regions we are hoping to visit? What are some possible choirs with whom you might arrange shared concerts?

- Beyond expenses, what would your fee/percentage be for this tour?

- If I can find a better airfare, can we hire you to make all of the other arrangements?

- Can you share some examples of publicity you have generated for your concerts? Print articles? Radio/television ads and teasers? What means of advertising have you found to be most effective in the cities/regions we want to visit?

- We will travel with fifty-five members. How many complimentary trips (for conductor, assistant conductor, chaperones, etc.) would you include for the price you're quoting?

A choir tour offers countless group-learning opportunities that are simply not possible in the classroom or rehearsal hall. Together, the chorus experiences these cherished "aha" learning moments that inevitably mature us both as singers and as people.

Perhaps the most valuable aspect of touring with your men is the renewed musical camaraderie and the fortified trust between them and you. Why does such bonding occur on the road and not in the usual rehearsal and performance space? Touring, like nothing else I have experienced in my musical career, promotes solidarity among singers. It is experiences such as flying together, endless bus rides, exotic cuisine, a tour guide whose accent no one can understand; it's getting caught unprepared in a heavy rainstorm or being stuck by the side of the road while a tire is changed; it's because the stage went black during Ron Jeffers' *I Have Had Singing* and yet even in total darkness not a single note was missed; and it's because of a pothole, a drum circle, and a performance in an unbearably hot church. It's times like these that bring us closer as peers and as musicians. On tour, we learn to trust each other.

Performance—of any kind and in any place—is the sharing of a mastered product. It is also inherently a transient art form. We can keep it close to home or take it to far-off places. Wherever we sing, whether it be a classroom, school auditorium, house of worship, or street corner, our voices carry us into the hearts and minds of others.

It is "In Tradition, Camaraderie and Musical Excellence," the mantra of the University of Michigan Men's Glee Club, that I say once again to male choirs and their leaders: sing on, brothers, sing on!

Michigan State University Men's Glee Club 2007 tour to Italy
After performance in Mantova

APPENDIX A
ORGANIZATIONS AND ASSOCIATIONS

AMERICAN CHORAL DIRECTORS ASSOCIATION
www.acda.org

The American Choral Directors Association maintains an active program for male choirs. The mission statement of the National Repertoire and Standards Committee on Male Choirs is to promote the best in male choir singing in America by helping male choirs and their directors gain access to repertoire, resources, and communication.

http://acda.org/page.asp?page=malechoir

This is the webpage specific to male choirs and includes the following subject headings: Mission Statement, Standards, Repertoire List, Resources, Leadership, and Male Choir Forum.

ASSOCIATED MALE CHORUSES OF AMERICA
http://amcofa-sing.org

Provides information and links to male choruses mainly throughout the midwestern United States. Scholarship application and "Big Sing" information also are provided online.

BARBERSHOP HARMONY SOCIETY / SOCIETY FOR THE PRESERVATION AND ENCOURAGEMENT OF BARBER SHOP QUARTET SINGING IN AMERICA, INC.
www.barbershop.org

Founded by Owen C. Cash in 1938, SPEBSQSA promotes barbershop harmony among men of all ages. As of 2007, nearly 30,000 men in the United States and Canada were members of this organization, whose focus is on a cappella music. The international headquarters was in Kenosha, Wisconsin, for fifty years before moving to Nashville, Tennessee, in 2007.

CHORAL NET
http://choralnet.org

This site, which is connected to the ACDA and can be reached by a link from the ACDA website, is widely used by choral professionals at every level and offers a vast array of resources. Forums, repertoire lists, program management and technology tools, merchant information, and a plethora of other subjects are addressed. Pages are updated regularly and visitors can easily post queries.

GALA: GAY AND LESBIAN ASSOCIATION OF CHORUSES, INC.
www.galachoruses.org

GALA Choruses helps to cultivate artistic development of nearly 8,000 choristers from around the world. GALA offers leadership workshops, choral festivals, and administrative support and funds new choral works and youth-related activities. There is also an online resource tool, including a music library.

INTERCOLLEGIATE MEN'S CHORUSES
http://www.imci.us

Founded in 1915, the Intercollegiate Men's Choruses association has strived to promote quality men's chorus singing and music. Its membership is composed of secondary school all-male choruses and university men's glee clubs. Associate memberships are also open to interested individuals and community and professional ensembles.

MALE CHOIR INTERNATIONAL INDEX
http://kvam.est.is/choirlink

This online resource provides links to men's choruses around the globe. Headings include Barbershop, Academic, Cathedral, Gregorian Chant, Synagogue, and Boys Choirs.

MUSICA
www.musicanet.org

This is a virtual choral library. The goal of Musica's library project is to list every choral work ever published.

SINGERS.COM
http://singers.com/choral/menschoir

Provides information and links to men's choirs around the world.

SUBITO
http://Subito.od.se

Subito is the online library of Orphei Drängar, the renowned Swedish male choir. This website boasts that "Subito is the world's largest catalogue of music for male-voice choirs."

NATIONAL LIBRARY OF MEN'S CHORAL MUSIC
http://camerata.com/library.php

Established in 1988 by the Washington Men's Camerata, there are more than 1,500 titles in this collection. Many works come from the men's choral music collections of Yale University, the Yale Institute of Sacred Music, and Georgetown University. In this library are hidden treasures, including original works and arrangements for men's chorus by Charles Ives, Marshall Bartholomew, and Fenno Heath.

APPENDIX B
TOOLS FOR TEACHING SIGHT-SINGING

ESSENTIAL SIGHT-SINGING VOLUME 1: MALE VOICES
Emily Crocker and John Leavitt
Hal Leonard 08744701

ESSENTIAL SIGHT-SINGING VOLUME 2: MALE VOICES
Emily Crocker and John Leavitt
Hal Leonard 08745344

KEYS TO SIGHT READING SUCCESS: SING A CAPPELLA TB/TBB
Six Songs with Preparatory Exercises
TB and TBB versions of each song
Composed by Lou Williams-Wimberly
Alliance Music Publications AMC 2015

KEYS TO SIGHT READING SUCCESS BOOK 4
90 EASY THREE-PART EXERCISES (SSA/TTB/SAB)
Composed by John Hemmenway
Alliance Music Publications AMC 2004

KEYS TO SIGHT READING SUCCESS BOOK 3
125 Moderate Two-Part Exercises (Bass Clef)
Edited by Marsha Carlisle
Alliance Music Publications AMC 2003B

ONE-MINUTE SIGHT SINGING (MULTIPLE LEVELS AVAILABLE)
All exercises provided in both treble and bass clef
Holly Shaw-Slabbinck and Ronald Slabbinck
Neil A. Kjos Music Co.

SIGHTREADING MANUALS: TB/TTB

Junior High School

Beginner (102), **Intermediate** (202), **Advanced** (302)

High School

Beginner (402), **Intermediate** (502), **Advanced** (602)

Thomas Stokes

Musical Resources, Toledo, Ohio

SIGHT SINGING MADE ACCESSIBLE, READABLE, TEACHABLE

SMART Volume 1

Exercises written in unison octaves in treble and bass clef for flexible use with mixed, tenor-bass, or treble choirs

Composed by Denise Eaton

Alliance Music Publications AMC 2011

SIGHT SINGING MADE ACCESSIBLE, READABLE, TEACHABLE

SMART MINOR

Exercises written in unison octaves in treble and bass clef for flexible use with mixed, tenor-bass, or treble choirs

Composed by Denise Eaton

Alliance Music Publications AMC 2014

SONGS FOR SIGHT SINGING: HIGH SCHOOL TB/TTB

Southern Music Co. #B371

Arranged by Henry/Jones/Whitlock

90 DAYS TO SIGHT READING SUCCESS

Alliance Music Publishing AMC2010

Stan McGill and H. Morris Stevens, Jr.

APPENDIX C
FURTHER READING ON WORKING WITH ADOLESCENT MALE VOICES

Barham, Terry J. and Darolyne L. Nelson. *The Boy's Changing Voice*. Miami: Belwin Mills, 1991.

Cooksey, John M. "The development of continuing, eclectic theory for the training and cultivation of the junior high school male changing voice." *Choral Journal* 18, nos. 2-5: 1977-78.

_____. *Working with Adolescent Voices*. St. Louis, MO: Concordia Publishing House, 1999.

Cooper, Irvin O. and Karl O. Kuersteiner. *Teaching junior high school music: general music and the vocal program*. 2nd ed. Conway, AK: Cambiata Press, 1973.

Killian, Janice. "A Description of Vocal Maturation among Fifth and Sixth Grade Boys." *Journal of Research in Music Education* 47, no. 4, 1999: 357-369.

Swanson, Frederick J. *The Male Singing Voice Ages Eight to Eighteen*. Cedar Rapids, IA: Laurance Press, 1977.

APPENDIX D
10 SAMPLE CONCERT PROGRAMS FOR MALE CHOIRS

UNIVERSITY OF MICHIGAN MEN'S GLEE CLUB
DR. JERRY BLACKSTONE, CONDUCTOR

Laudes atque Carmina   Albert A. Stanley

This is a university-specific song that has opened University of Michigan Men's Glee Club concerts for over 100 years.

Shakespeare Songs (1984)   Theodore Morrison
    When daisies pied
    Take, O take those lips away
    Full fathom five

Spaséñiye sodélal   Pavel Chesnokov

Quatre Petites Prieres
de Saint Francois D'Assise   Francis Poulenc
    Salut, Dame Sainte
    Seigneur, Je Vous en Prie

Indianas No. 2   Carlos Guastavino
    Eduardo Belgrano
    Sino

Reconciliation   Stephen Chatman

Dance   David Conte

University of Wisconsin-Eau Claire Statesmen
Dr. Gary Schwartzhoff, conductor

I

Trösterin Musik	Anton Bruckner
Cantate Domino	Hans Leo Hassler
Ubi Caritas	Ola Gjeilo
Ave Maria	Franz Biebl

II

Alleluia	Randall Thompson
Aleluia Brasileira Manuscript	Ralph Manuel/Gary Schwartzhoff
La Tarde Manuscript	Carlos Guastavino
Adiós, Corazón De Almendra Manuscript	Carlos Guastavino

III

Arms of an Angel	Sarah McLachlan/Eric Hagmann
Insomniac The Innocent Men	arr. Eric Hagmann

IV

All Through the Night	arr. Mack Wilberg
When I Fall in Love	arr. James Mulholland
Bonse Aba	arr. Andrew Fischer
Ramkali	arr. Ethan Sperry
Pirate Song	Tim Jones
If You're Out There	John Legend/Joe Holtan
I Have Had Singing	Ron Jeffers

V

Songs of the University
Hail University
Alma Mater
Fight Song

BALDWIN-WALLACE COLLEGE MEN'S CHORUS
FRANK BIANCHI, CONDUCTOR
WINTER CONCERT

Salmo 150	Ernani Aguiar
Cantate Domino	Hans Leo Hassler
I Will Be Earth	Gwyneth Walker

Small Ensemble
(Selections announced from the stage)

Ol' Man River	Jerome Kern
	arr. Russell Robinson
Hallelujah	Leonard Cohen
	arr. Ethan Sperry
Manly Men	Kurt Knecht
I Am That Man	Mark Hayes

Combined with the Women's Chorus

Homeland	Z. Randall Stroope

CENTRAL BUCKS HIGH SCHOOL-WEST MEN'S CHOIR
DR. JOSEPH OHRT, CONDUCTOR
2008 ACDA EASTERN DIVISION CONVENTION

The Year Begins to Be Ripe from *Song Books, Volume 1* Unison, percussive piano	John Cage
Adoramus Te	Giovanni Pierluigi da Palestrina
"Der Herr Segne Euch" from *Cantata No. 196*	J.S. Bach

Thirteen Ways of Looking at a Blackbird

1. *Among twenty snowy mountains*	Matthew Harris
2. *I was of three minds*	Jonathan Miller
3. *The blackbird whirled in the autumn winds*	Libby Larsen
4. *A man and a woman*	Stephen Hatfield
5. *I do not know which to prefer*	Stephen Paulus
6. *Icicles filled the long window*	Eleanor Daley
7. *O thin men of Haddam*	Jaakko Mäntyjärvi
8. *I know noble accents*	Daniel Gawthrop
9. *When the blackbird flew out of sight*	Rollo Dilworth
10. *At the sight of blackbirds*	Meuryn Hughes
11. *He rode over Connecticut*	Ola Gjeilo
12. *The river is moving*	David Conte
13. *It was evening all afternoon*	Tarik O'Regan

Commissioned for the
Central Bucks High School-West Men's Choir
unpublished manuscript

Ramkali	arr. by Ethan Sperry

PLANO [TEXAS] SENIOR HIGH SCHOOL MEN'S CHOIR
DERRICK BROOKINS, CONDUCTOR
SPRING CONCERT

If Music Be the Food of Love	David Dickau
The Finlandia Hymn	Jean Sibelius
O Susannah!	Stephen Foster arr. Jonathan Crutchfield
Amor Vittorioso	Giovanni Gastoldi arr. Leininger
For the Fallen	Mike Sammes
What Shall We Do With a Drunken Sailor	arr. Marshall Bartholomew

WASHINGTON MEN'S CAMERATA
FRANK ALBINDER, CONDUCTOR
JUNE 2011

I.

Heleluyan: Muskogee Indian Chant	arr. Jerry Ulrich/William Skoog
Three Native American Melodies	Alan Stringer

      Adapted from Native American Sources

      1. The Morning Star

      2. Dust of the Red Wagon

      3. Song of the Dove

II.

Missa Brevis III: Kyrie	Ernani Aguiar
Salmo 150	Ernani Aguiar

III.

Away From the Roll of the Sea	Allister MacGillivray
	arr. Diane Loomer
Jonah's Song	Peter Schickele

IV.

Preces sem Palavras	Heitor Villa-Lobos
Jing-ga-lye-ya	Bruce Sled

V.

There Is a Balm in Gilead	arr. William L. Dawson
Didn' my Lord delivuh Daniel?	arr. William Bradley Roberts

Intermission

VI.

Men of the future, stand	St. Albans School Hymn
Down in the Valley	Kentucky Folk Tune arr. George Mead
Aura Lee	George R. Poulton arr. Alice Parker & Robert Shaw
Old Man Noah	arr. Marshall Bartholomew
Just My Imagination	Norman J. Whitfield & Barrett Strong, arr. Mac Huff
There Is Nothing Like a Dame	Richard Rodgers arr. William Stickles

VII.

El Guatecano	Emílio Murillo arr. Demetrio Haralambis
Home on the Range	arr. Greg Gilpin
Rio Què Pasas Llorando	Alcides Briceño arr. Leonard de Paur

VIII.

Night and Day	Cole Porter arr. Walter Scotson
All the Things You Are	Jerome Kern arr. William Stickles
Slap That Bass	George Gershwin arr. William Stickles

IX.

Stopping by Woods on a Snowy Evening	Randall Thompson
Ching-a-Ring Chaw	Adapted by Aaron Copland arr. Irving Fine

UNIVERSITY SCHOOL GLEE CLUB
JONATHAN PALANT, CONDUCTOR
ENGLAND TOUR 2006

The Last Words of David	Randall Thompson
Adoramus te, Christe	G.P. Palestrina
"*Wie will ich mich freuen*" from *Cantata No. 146*	J.S. Bach
The Prayer	Damijan Močnik
Rex tremendae	Jonathan Palant
Loveliest of Trees, the Cherry Now	Richard Nance

US Males
(Selections announced from the stage)

Lambscapes — Eric Lane Barnes
- I. Gregorian Chant
- II. Handel
- III. Schubert
- IV. Verdi
- V. Gospel

Bridge Over Troubled Water — Simon & Garfunkel
arr. Kirby Shaw

Nkosi Sikelel' iAfrika — Enoch Sontonga/arr. Larentz-Jones

MIAMI UNIVERSITY GLEE CLUB
DR. ETHAN SPERRY, CONDUCTOR

Adoro Te Devote	Gregorian Chant
"Kyrie" from *Missa Brevis*	Healey Willan
"Gloria" from *Missa Mater Patris*	Josquin des Prez
Incantatio Maris Aestuosi	Veljo Tormis
Pallanda, Indian Raga	arr. Ethan Sperry
"Wedding Qawwali" from *Bombay Dreams*	A. R. Rahman arr. Ethan Sperry

MIAMI UNIVERSITY
DR. JEREMY D. JONES, DIRECTOR
SPRING 2012

El Yivneh Hagalil arr. Peter Sozio	Hebrew Folk Song
Spaséñiye sodélal, Op. 25, No. 5	Pavel Chesnokov
Ramkali	Indian Raga arr. Ethan Sperry
Night, Veiled Night Commissioned by the MU Glee Club for their 2012 IMC National Seminar Performance	Anthony J. Maglione
Demon in My View	Jeffrey T. Horvath
"Dance" from *Invocation and Dance*	David Conte
The Last Words of David	Randall Thompson
Beautiful Savior	arr. F. Melius Christiansen
We Shall Walk Through the Valley in Peace	arr. William Appling
Sometimes I Feel Like a Motherless Child	arr. Fenno Heath

Traditional School Songs

Johnny Schmoeker	Clyde Dengler and Vivian R. Walton
The Miami University Fight Song & Alma Mater	Raymond Burke
A Parting Blessing	J. Jerome Williams

FOREST MEADOW JUNIOR HIGH SCHOOL MEN'S CHOIR
KARI GILBERTSON, CONDUCTOR
SPRING CONCERT

Sing To the Lord	Emily Crocker
Colorado Trail	Jennifer Scoggin
Battle Above the Clouds	John Parker & Vicki Tucker Courtney
O, Mr. Moon	arr. Joshua Shank
Bidi Bom	arr. David Eddleman
Joshua!	arr. Kirby Shaw
She Walks in Beauty	Laura Farnell
Seize the Day	Alan Menken, arr. Emerson

APPENDIX E
50 RECOMMENDED TITLES
FOR ADOLESCENT MALE VOICES

A La Nanita Nana (Spanish Carol)
Dan Davison
TB, two-part, piano, 2 violins
and opt. guitar
Walton Music
08501548

Amani (A Song for Peace)
Papoulis, Jim
arr. Francisco Núñez
SSA, percussion
Boosey & Hawkes
48005167

Bashana Haba'ah
Hirsh, Nurit
arr. Henry Leck
two-part, piano
Hal Leonard
08602199

Bidi Bom
Eddleman, David
TTB, two-part, piano
Carl Fischer
CM8799

Cantate Domino
Cobb, Nancy Hill
two-part, piano
Santa Barbara Music
SBMP282

Cantate Domino
Farnell, Laura
TTB, piano
Hal Leonard
08747425

Children, Go Where I Send Thee
Crocker, Emily
TTB, piano
Jenson
47103041

Cindy
arr. Michael Scott
TB
piano and guitar
Warner Brothers
SV8849

Colorado Trail
Moore, Donald
TTB, piano
BriLee Music
BL162

Come Travel with Me
Farthing, Scott
TTB, piano
Hal Leonard
08501432

Cover Me With the Night
Ramsey, Andrea
TTB, piano
Alliance
AMP0766

Cripple Creek
arr. Emily Crocker
TB, piano
Hal Leonard
08551839

El Aire Lloro
Núñez, Francisco J.
TB, piano
Boosey & Hawkes
48020740

Festival Sanctus
Leavitt, John
TTB, piano
Alfred
28659

Hey, Good Lookin'
Williams, Hank, arr. Jay Althouse
TBB, piano (opt. track)
Alfred
27167

Homeland
Stroope, Z. Randall
TBB, piano (opt. brass and perc.)
Colla Voce Music
48-96810

I'm Bound Away
arr. Donald Moore
TTB, piano
Alfred
SV9313

Jamaica Farewell!
(Jamaican folk song)
Nelson, Bradley
TB, percussion, opt. synth
Neil A. Kjos
5570

Jesu, Joy of Man's Desiring
Bach, J.S., arr. Siltman
CBB, opt. handbells
Cambiata Press
M97687

Jonah
Dilworth, Rollo
TTB, piano
Hal Leonard
08744464

Jubilate Deo
Mozart, W.A., arr. Linda Spevacek
TB, piano
Heritage
15/1589H

Kyrie Eleison
Davison, Dan
TB, piano
Walton Music
08501555

Let There Be Peace on Earth
Miller, Sy and Jill Jackson, arr. Hawley Ades
two-part, SAB, SSA, piano
Shawnee
35012617

Medieval Gloria
Singh, Vijay
TB, unaccompanied, opt. hand drum
Warner Brothers
OCT9614

Medieval Kyrie
Singh, Vijay
TB, unaccompanied, opt. hand drum and
finger cymbals
BriLee Music
BL518

Medley for Christmas
arr. Bob Siltman
TB, unaccompanied
Cambiata Press
U978115

Mouth Music
Keane, Dolores and John Faulkner
SSA/TTB, drum
Earthsongs
M-28

My Bonnie Anne Marie
Parker, John and Vicki Tucker Courtney
T[T]B, flute
BriLee Music
BL630

Now Is the Time
Berry, Lon
TTB, piano (opt. track)
BriLee Music
BL 489

Passing By
Crocker, Emily
TTB, piano or unaccompanied
Hal Leonard
08551945

Red, Red Rose, A
Crocker, Emily
TTB, piano
Hal Leonard
08740102

Rest Not
Farnell, Laura
TB, piano
Hal Leonard
08552012

Rosalee
Perry, Dave and Jean
TTB, piano
Jenson
42318041

She Walks in Beauty
Farnell, Laura
TB, piano
Alliance
AMP0547

She's Like the Swallow
Farnell, Laura
TB, piano
Alliance
AMP0509

Shepherd's Spiritual
Moore, Donald
TB, piano (opt. tambourine)
BriLee Music
BL179

Shine on Me
arr. Rollo Dilworth
TTB, piano
Hal Leonard
08751307

Sing Me a Song of a Lad That Is Gone
Porterfield, Sherri
TTB, piano
Belwin
SV9003

Sinner Man
arr. Roger Emerson
TB, piano
Hal Leonard
08551784

Soldier's Hallelujah
Singh, Vijay
TB, unaccompanied
BriLee Music
BL137

Songs of the Road and the Sea
Farnell, Laura
TB, unaccompanied
Hal Leonard
08751154

Spirituals Medley
(African-American spirituals)
Berry, Lon
TTB, piano
BriLee Music
BL478

Sword of Bunker Hill
Armstrong, Matthew
TTB, piano
Carl Fischer
CM9205

Tell My Father
Wildhorn, Frank, arr. Andrea Ramsey
TTB, piano and solo violin
Hal Leonard
02501096

The Noble Son
(Visi Kauli Nogurusi)
arr. Audrey Snyder
TTB, piano
Hal Leonard
08703269

'Til the Walls Come Down
Berry, Lon
TTB, piano
BriLee Music
BL434

To Work Upon the Railway
Rentz, Earlene
TTB, piano
Heritage
15/2414H

Tollite Hostias
(from the Christmas Oratorio)
Saint-Saëns, Camille, arr. Linda Mulder
TTB, unaccompanied
BriLee Music
BL193

Turtle Dove
(British folk song)
arr. Ken Berg
TTB, piano
Walton Music
08501726

Yellow Bird
Luboff, Norman
arr. Dan Davison
TB, piano, flute, opt. perc.
Walton Music
08501610

APPENDIX F
100 RECOMMENDED TITLES FOR MALE CHOIRS

Absalon, fili mi
des Prez, Josquin
arr. Jameson Marvin
TTBB, unaccompanied
Broude Brothers
CR38

Aftonen
Alfven, Hugo
arr. Norman Luboff
TTBB, unaccompanied
Walton Music Corp.
8501511

Agincourt Song, The
(English song, circa 1415)
Willan, Healy
TTBB, piano
Oxford Univerity Press
9780193852020

Alleluia
Thompson, Randall
TTBB, unaccompanied
E.C. Schirmer
2312.ecs

Amo, Amas, I love a lass
(early English glee)
arr. Marshall Bartholomew
TBB, unaccompanied
Theodore Presser Co.
352-00133

Amor de mi Alma
Stroope, Z. Randall
TTBB, piano
Walton Music Corp.
8501615

At the River
(hymn tune)
Copland, Aaron
TTBB, piano
Boosey & Hawkes
48003500

Ave Maria (Angelus Domini)
Biebl, Franz
TTB/TTBB, unaccompanied
Hinshaw Music, Inc.
HMC1253

Awakening, The
Martin, Joseph
TTBB, piano
Shawnee Press
35001492

Away From the Roll of the Sea
MacGillivray, Allister
arr. Diane Loomer
TTBB, piano
Cypress Publications
CP1028

Ballad of Little Musgrave and Lady Barnard
Britten, Benjamin
TTBB, piano
Boosey & Hawkes
48008878

Barb'ra Allen
Marvin, Jameson
TTBB, unaccompanied
Neil A. Kjos Music Co.
5577.kj

Bashana Haba'ah
Hirsh, Nurit
arr. John Leavitt
TTBB, piano/opt. clarinet, violin, cello, bass
Hal Leonard
8740577

Battle Hymn of the Republic
Steffe, William
arr. Peter Wilhousky
TTBB, piano (opt. band or orch.)
Carl Fischer
CM6778

Beati Mortui Op. 115 no. 1
Mendelssohn, Felix
ed. Michael Weber
TTBB, unaccompanied
Alliance Music Publishing
AMP0311

Behold Man
Nelson, Ron
TTBB, unaccompanied
Boosey & Hawkes
48003432

Betelehemu
(Nigerian Christmas song)
Olatunji, Via
arr. Wendell Whalum
TTBB, drums ad lib.
Lawson Gould
LG52647

Blow Ye the Trumpet
Mechem, Kirke
TTBB, piano/organ or orch.
G. Schirmer
50481989

Brothers, Sing On!
Grieg, Edvard
ed. Howard McKinney
TTBB, unaccompanied
Belwin
FEC06927

Cantate Domino
Hassler, Hans Leo
TTBB, unaccompanied
ECS Publishing
68.ecs

Canticle
Conte, David
TTBB div., piano 4-hands
ECS Publishing
4170.ecs

Cantique de Jean Racine Op. 11
Fauré, Gabriel
arr. K. Lee Scott
TTBB, piano opt. violin
Hinshaw Music, Inc.
HMC714

Carnival Song
Piston, Walter
TBB, piano 4-hands reduction/brass
Associated Music Publishers
50229390

Daemon Irrepit Callidus
Orbán, Gyorgy
TTBB, unaccompanied
Hinshaw Music, Inc.
HMC1829

Danny Boy
(Irish folk song)
arr. Jameson Marvin
TTBB, unaccompanied
Mark Foster
MF1503

De Animals A-Comin'
(spiritual)
Bartholomew, Marshall
TB, piano
G. Schirmer
50303230

Dirait-on
Lauridsen, Morten
TTBB, piano
Peer Music Classical
61880-120

Dona Nobis Pacem
Gregorio, Joseph
TTBBB, unaccompanied
ECS Publishing
6511.ecs

Down by the Sally Gardens
(old Irish air)
Mishkin, Henry
TTBB, unaccompanied
ECS Publishing
2153.ecs

Down in the Valley
(Kentucky folk tune)
arr. George Mead
TTBB, piano
Galaxy
1.1716

Dravidian Dithyramb
Paranjoti, Victor
arr. Donald Patriquin
TTBB, unaccompanied
Earthsongs
M-24

Dulaman
McGlynn, Michael
TTBB, unaccompanied
www.anuna.ie

El Yivneh Hagalil
(Hebrew folk song)
Sozio, Peter
TTBB, unaccompanied
Unicorn
14010030

Ev'ry Time I Feel the Spirit
(traditional spiritual)
Hogan, Moses
arr. James Rodde
TTBB, unaccompanied
Hal Leonard
8744443

Fight the Good Fight Op. 54 No. 5
Gardner, John
TTBB, piano
Oxford Univerity Press
9780193859456

For the Fallen
Sammes, Mike
TTBB, piano or organ
Banks Music Publishing
8300583

Gentle Annie
Foster, Stephen
arr. Robert Shaw and Alice Parker
TTBB, piano or guitar
Lawson Gould
LG00859

Goin' Home
Dvorak, Antonin
arr. Diane Loomer
TB, unaccompanied
Cypress Publications
CP1055

Got a Mind to Do Right
Morrow, David
TTBB, unaccompanied
Lawson Gould
LG52502

Grace
(early American melody)
Hayes, Mark
TTBB, piano/opt. orch
Beckenhorst Press
BP1599

Hard Times Come Again No More
Foster, Stephen
arr. Donald Moore
TTBB, unaccompanied, opt. string bass
Belwin
SV8938

Hark, I Hear Harps Eternal
(traditional hymn)
arr. Alice Parker
TTBB, unaccompanied
Lawson Gould
28499

He Never Failed Me Yet
Ray, Robert, arr. Keith Christopher
TTBB, piano
Hal Leonard
8745113

Heaven
Thomas, Andre
TTBB, piano
Mark Foster
35009139

Home on the Range
Higley, Brewster
arr. Greg Gilpin
TTBB, unaccompanied
Shawnee Press
C0325

Homeland
Holst, Gustav
arr. Z. Randall Stroope
TTBB, piano
Colla Voce
48-96690

How Can I Keep From Singing?
(Quaker hymn)
arr. Gwyneth Walker
TTBB, piano
ECS Publishing
6336.ecs

Hush! Somebody's Callin' My Name (traditional spiritual)
Dennard, Brazeal
TTBB, unaccompanied
Shawnee Press
C0278

I Am in Need of Music
Brunner, David
TTBB, piano
Boosey & Hawkes
48019728

I Have Had Singing
Jeffers, Ron
TTBB, unaccompanied
Earthsongs
S-193

In Remembrance (from 'Requiem')
Daley, Eleanor
TTBB, unaccompanied
Rhythmic Trident Music
RTCA-011

Inveni David
Bruckner, Anton
TTBB, 4 trombones
C.F. Peters Corp.
EP6318

Invocation
Debussy, Claude
TTBB, piano or orch.
Choudens
C0003

Invocation and Dance
Conte, David
TTBB, 4-hand piano, percussion /
opt. orch.
ECS Publishing
4179.ecs

Kolm mul oli kaunist sona
(Three Words of Beauty)
Tormis, Veljo
TTBB, flute
Edition 49 (import)
M204302270

Last Letter Home
Hoiby, Lee
TBB, unaccompanied
Schott
49016738

Last Words of David, The
Thompson, Randall
TTBB, piano/orch. or band
ECS Publishing
2154.ecs

Loch Lomond (Scottish air)
Vaughan Williams, Ralph
TTBB, unaccompanied
Galaxy
1.5215

Lowlands (American sea shanty)
Shaw, Robert and Alice Parker
TTBB/bar. solo, unaccompanied
Lawson Gould
LG51059

Lux aeterna
Schmidt, Brian
TTBB, unaccompanied
Walton Music
8501670

Lux Aurumque
Whitacre, Eric
TTBB, unaccompanied
Walton Music
8501528

Mogami River Boat Song
(Mogamigawa funa uta)
arr. Osamu Shimizu
TTBB, unaccompanied
Earthsongs
S-300

O Magnum Mysterium
Lauridsen, Morten
TTBB, unaccompanied
Peer Music
62016-120

O My Luve's Like a Red, Red Rose
Clausen, René
TTBB, piano, violin, cello
Mark Foster
35015689

O Sacrum Convivium
Viadana, Lodovico
ed. Archibald T. Davidson
TTBB, unaccompanied
ECS Publishing
78.ecs

Pasture, The (No. 2 from Frostiana)
Thompson, Randall
TBB, piano
ECS Publishing
2181.ecs

Prayer of the Children
Bestor, Kurt
arr. Andrea Klouse
TTBB, unaccompanied
Warner Bros.
CH96166

Promised Land
Kirk, Theron
TB, unaccompanied
Oxford Univerity Press
9780193860506

Quatre Petites Prieres de Saint Francois D'Assise
Poulenc, Francis
TTBB, unaccompanied
Editions Salabert, Inc.
50431270

Rainbow 'Round My Shoulder
(chain gang song)
arr. Robert DeCormier
TTBB, percussion
Lawson Gould
LG51757

Ride the Chariot (spritual)
arr. William Henry Smith
TTBB/tenor solo, unaccompanied
Neil A. Kjos Music Co.
1102.kj

Salmo 150
Aguiar, Ernani
TTBB, unaccompanied
Earthsongs
S-240

Shenandoah
arr. James Erb
TTBBB, unaccompanied
Lawson Gould
LG52677

Song of Democracy
Hanson, Howard
arr. Maurice Ford
TTBB, piano
Carl Fischer LLC
O4262

Song of Peace
Persichetti, Vincent
TTBB, piano
Theodore Presser Co.
362-00130

Songs of a Young Man
Nance, Richard
TTBB, piano
Hinshaw Music, Inc.
HMC807

Soon Ah Will Be Done
arr. William Dawson
TTBB, unaccompanied
Neil A. Kjos Music Co.
T101a

Spaseniye sodelal
(Salvation Is Created)
Chesnokov, Pavel
TTBB(B), unaccompanied
Musica Russica
Cn176MC

Stars Are With the Voyager
Daley, Eleanor
TTBB, piano
Rhythmic Trident Music
RTCA-003

Stars I Shall Find
Dickau, David
TTBB, piano
Walton Music
8501605

Stomp Your Foot
Copland, Aaron
TTBB, piano duet
Boosey & Hawkes
48003318

Stopping By Woods on a Snowy Evening
(No. 6 from Frostiana)
Thompson, Randall
TTB, piano or band or orch.
ECS Publishing
2182.ecs

Sure on This Shining Night
(from Nocturnes)
Lauridsen, Morten
TTBB, piano
Peer Music
229299

Tell My Father (from *The Civil War: An American Musical*)
Wildhorn, Frank
arr. Andrea Ramsey
TTB
Piano, opt. violin
Hal Leonard
2501096

Testament of Freedom
Thompson, Randall
TTBB, piano or band or orch.
ECS Publishing
2118.ecs

Think On Me
Mulholland, James
TTBB, piano
Colla Voce
20-96905

Thou Didst Delight My Eyes
Finzi, Gerald
TTBB, unaccompanied
Boosey & Hawkes
48003460

Tshotsholoza
(South African freedom song)
Ames, Jeffrey
TTBB/tenor solo, congas and djembe
Walton Music
8501546

Ubi Caritas
Gjeilo, Ola
TTBB, unaccompanied
Walton Music
8501701

Varjele, Jumala, Soasta
(God Protect Us From War)
Tormis, Veljo
TTBB, tam-tam
Fennica Gehrman

Vive L'Amour (traditional American)
Shaw, Robert and Alice Parker
TTBB, unaccompanied
Lawson Gould
LG51026

We Rise Again
Dubinsky, Leon
arr. Stephen Smith
TTBB, piano
Cypress Publications
CP1141

We Shall Walk Through the Valley in Peace (spiritual)
Appling, William
TTBB, unaccompanied
World Lib
2328

Western Songs

(American folk songs)

Wagner, Roger

TTBB, piano

Lawson Gould

LG52575

What Shall We Do With a Drunken Sailor (English sea shanty)

Shaw, Robert and Alice Parker

TTBB, unaccompanied

Lawson Gould

LF51053

Widerspruch

Schubert, Franz

English version by Alice Parker

TTBB, piano

Lawson Gould

LG00513

Witness (traditional spiritual)

Hogan, Moses

TTBB, unaccompanied

Hal Leonard

8743357

Workin' (Waitin') for the Dawn of Peace (Civil War song)

Jeffers, Ron

TTBB, unaccompanied

Earthsongs

M-01

Zikr

Sperry, Ethan

TTBB, percussion

Earthsongs

S-254

Zion's Walls

Copland, Aaron

arr. Glenn Koponen

TTBB, piano

Boosey & Hawkes

48003922

BIOGRAPHIES OF CONTRIBUTING AUTHORS

Steven Albaugh is the head of the choral/vocal program at Rosemount High School in Rosemount, Minnesota. He has also held teaching and conducting positions in Center Point and Cedar Rapids, Iowa and at Eagan High School, Eagan, Minnesota. Active in the American Choral Director's Association in both Iowa and Minnesota, Albaugh served as chairperson of the Iowa Choral Director's Association Summer Convention and as president of ACDA of Minnesota.

Christopher Aspaas is associate professor of music at St. Olaf College, Northfield, Minnesota. There, he conducts both the Viking Chorus and the Chapel Choir and teaches choral conducting, choral literature, and private applied voice. Aspaas is also music director of the Twin Cities' choral ensemble Magnum Chorum.

Peter Bagley is professor emeritus of music and special assistant to the dean of the School of Fine Arts at The University of Connecticut. He taught public school music in Greenwich, Connecticut, and prior to his appointment as director of choral activities at UConn, was professor of music at the State University of New York at New Paltz.

Christine Bass taught choral music at Cherry Hill High School West, Cherry Hill, New Jersey, for more than twenty years. She serves as guest conductor and clinician nationally and has presented workshops for NJEA, NJMEA, ACDA, and WCC. Bass served as chair of Repertoire and Standards for Male Choirs of the New Jersey American Choral Directors Association. Her DVDs "Vocal Transformation for Secondary School Choirs" and "Where the Boys Are" are published by Hal Leonard Corporation.

Frank Bianchi taught secondary choral music in Medina, Ohio, prior to his faculty appointment at Baldwin Wallace University Conservatory of Music. He is founder and conductor of the BW Men's Chorus and served for six years as conductor of the Cleveland Orchestra Youth Chorus. Bianchi was also assistant conductor of the Cleveland Orchestra Chorus for two seasons.

Jerry Blackstone is director of choirs and chair of the Conducting Department at the University of Michigan School of Music, Theatre & Dance, where he conducts the Chamber Choir, teaches conducting at the graduate level, and administers a choral program of eleven choirs. Blackstone received two GRAMMY® Awards for his work as chorusmaster for the critically acclaimed Naxos recording of William Bolcom's monumental *Songs of Innocence and of Experience*. He also serves as conductor and music director of the University Musical Society Choral Union, a large community/university chorus that frequently appears with the Detroit Symphony Orchestra.

Kerry P. Brennan is headmaster of The Roxbury Latin School. Previously headmaster of Manhattan's Collegiate School and Director of Cleveland's University School, he has directed male choruses at the collegiate, secondary, and elementary levels. He currently serves as associate conductor of Mastersingers USA, a 100-voice male chorus, and is founder and director of The Sly Voxes, a Boston-based sixteen-man a cappella group.

Derrick Brookins has taught choral music in the Plano [Texas] Independent School District for nearly twenty years. For fifteen years, Brookins was a member of the Moses Hogan Chorale. His choirs have appeared at numerous state and national conventions.

Lesley French Childs, M.D., is assistant professor of otolaryngology—head and neck surgery, and a laryngologist in the Clinical Center for Voice Care at the University of Texas Southwestern Medical Center. She completed both medical school and residency at Vanderbilt University School of Medicine and did her laryngology fellowship at the New York Head and Neck Institute in Manhattan.

Dennis Coleman is artistic director of the Seattle Men's Chorus, a position he has held since 1981, and conductor of the Seattle Women's Chorus. He is a founding board member of Gala Choruses Inc., and served for six years on the Chorus America board of directors. Coleman is also minister of music at the First Congregational Church of Bellevue, Washington.

Karl Dent is professor of voice and choral studies at Texas Tech University, where he conducts the 55-voice male chorus, The Matador Singers. He formerly served on the music faculties of Hardin-Simmons University and The University of Texas at Dallas. As an oratorio and concert soloist, Dent has performed in major concert halls throughout the United States and around the world. His recording credits are extensive and include several albums on the TELARC label under the direction of Robert Shaw.

Rollo Dilworth is associate professor of choral music education and chair of the Music Education Department at the Temple University Boyer College of Music and Dance. Prior to his appointment at the Boyer College, Dilworth was on faculty at North Park University in Chicago for thirteen years, where he was director of choral activities and music education. Before teaching at the college level, he taught choral and general music at the middle school level in his native city of St. Louis, Missouri. More than 150 of his choral compositions and arrangements have been published—many of which are a part of the *Henry Leck Creating Artistry Choral Series* with Hal Leonard Corporation. Dilworth is a contributing author for the *Essential Elements for Choir* and the *Experiencing Choral Music* textbook series, both published by the Hal Leonard Corporation/Glencoe/McGraw-Hill Publications and for *Music Express!* Teachers Magazine. He authored a book of choral warm-ups for elementary and secondary choral ensembles titled *Choir Builders: Fundamental Vocal Techniques for General and Classroom Use.* Dilworth has co-authored another choral warm-up book titled *Choir Builders for Growing Voices.*

Laura Farnell taught for eight years at Boles Junior High in Arlington, Texas. In 2004, she received an Excellence in Education Award as the Arlington Independent School District's outstanding junior high teacher of the year. A prolific composer, Farnell is published by Alliance Music Publications, BriLee Music, Hal Leonard Corporation, Heritage Music, and Kjos Music Press.

Kari Gilbertson taught for fifteen years at Forest Meadow Junior High School in Richardson, Texas, before becoming the head choir director at Lake Highlands High School in Richardson. Gilbertson is a lead author on the new Hal Leonard/McGraw Hill choral textbook Voices in Concert. She is a contributing author to both the Glencoe textbook series *Experiencing Choral Music* and the McGraw-Hill elementary series *Spotlight on Music*, and is a regular presenter and clinician at choral conventions and festivals nationwide.

Amy Hamilton, MA, CCC-SLP, is a speech-language pathologist at the University of Texas Southwestern Medical Center specializing in assessing and treating voice disorders and working with the professional voice. Hamilton received vocology certification from the University of Iowa's Vocology Institute.

Thomas Jenrette retired in 2012 after thirty-three years as professor of music and direc-tor of choral activities at East Tennessee State University. Jenrette served as the American Choral Directors Association's southern division chair of Repertoire and Standards for Male Choirs from 2000 to 2006 and as Tennessee Repertoire and Standards chair from 1990 until 2000. In 2012, Jenrette received the Marshall Bartholomew Award "for sig-nificant contributions to the field of male chorus music" from the Intercollegiate Men's Choruses and the Lifetime Achievement Award from the Tennessee American Choral Directors Association.

Jefferson Johnson is director of choral activities at the University of Kentucky in Lexington, Kentucky, where he conducts the UK Chorale and UK Men's Chorus. He teaches advanced choral conducting, choral methods, and literature and directs the graduate program in choral music. In addition to his work at the University of Kentucky, Johnson is musical di-rector and conductor of the Lexington Singers, an auditioned community chorus of about 180 singers.

Jeremy D. Jones is assistant professor of music and director of choral activities at Miami University in Oxford, Ohio. There, he conducts the Collegiate Chorale and the Men's Glee Club, teaches courses in music education, and supervises student teachers. His research on male collegiate glee clubs led to publications in the *Choral Journal* and a presentation at the 2008 Intercollegiate Men's Choruses National Seminar.

Diane Loomer, C.M., recipient of the Order of Canada, was artistic director and founder of Chor Leoni Men's Choir (Vancouver, B.C.), co-founder and conductor emerita of Elektra Women's Choir, and founder and conductor of EnChor Chamber Choir. Loomer's choral compositions have been published and recorded internationally. She taught on the music faculty of the University of British Columbia and Douglas College. In 2011, Loomer was recipient of an honorary Doctorate of Letters degree from the University of British Columbia and in 2012 received the Queen Elizabeth II Diamond Jubilee Medal, as well as an honorary Doctorate of Fine Arts from Gustavus Adolphus College. She died in December 2012.

Fernando Malvar-Ruiz is the Litton-Lodal music director of The American Boychoir. He leads the choir annually in more than one hundred performances throughout the United States and tours with it internationally. A native of Spain, Malvar-Ruiz earned his undergraduate degree in piano performance and music theory from the Reál Conservatorio Superior de Música in Madrid and completed his Kodály certification in Kécskemet, Hungary, where he was awarded the Sharolta Kodály scholarship. He holds a master's degree in choral conducting from Ohio State University, and has completed all coursework toward a doctoral degree in musical arts from the University of Illinois.

Jameson Marvin is emeritus director of choral activities, senior lecturer on music at Harvard University (1978-2010). Under his baton, the Harvard Glee Club, Radcliffe Choral Society, and the Harvard-Radcliffe Collegium Musicum appeared at nine Eastern Division and seven National Conventions of the American Choral Directors Association, and the choral program at Harvard was named by *Classical Singer* magazine as the top collegiate choral program in the United States. Marvin's publication catalogue is extensive with nearly forty Renaissance editions and thirty folk song arrangements available for mixed, women, and men's choruses.

Ted Mau, M.D., Ph.D. is assistant professor of otolaryngology at the University of Texas Southwestern Medical Center. He is a graduate of Harvard Medical School and completed his residency at the University of California, San Francisco, and his fellowship at Vanderbilt University. Mau's area of focus is on voice disorders. His research interests include vocal fold tissue biomechanics, perceptual qualities of disordered voices, and surgical techniques for vocal fold medialization.

Alan McClung joined the University of North Texas College of Music faculty in 2002. He conducts UNT's Concert Choir, teaches undergraduate choral conducting and courses in secondary choral methods, and supervises student teachers. He is author of *Movable Tonic: A Sequenced Sight-Singing Method*, a GIA publication, and he is director of the Cambiata Institute of America for Early Adolescent Vocal Music, established on the campus of the University of North Texas in 2009.

Kevin Meidl is director of choirs and music department chair at Appleton West High School in Wisconsin and has taught at the junior high school level as well. He is the artistic director and principal conductor of the Appleton Boychoir, a treble choir of young boys, and conductor of the Badger State Girl Choir.

Francisco J. Núñez, a 2011 MacArthur Fellow, is a conductor, composer, music educator, and the founder of the award-winning Young People's Chorus of New York City, cited as a national model of artistic excellence and diversity under the Clinton, Bush, and Obama administrations. Núñez also leads the University Glee Club of New York City, its fifth conductor since the all-men's choir was established in 1894. He has received awards from ASCAP and the New York Choral Society, and was named La Sociedad Coral Latinoamericana's Man of the Year in 2009. His music and arrangements are published by Boosey & Hawkes.

Matthew Oltman is music director emeritus of the Grammy-award-winning male vocal ensemble Chanticleer. Oltman first joined Chanticleer in 1999 as a tenor and in 2004 was named assistant music director under Joseph Jennings, a post he held until his appointment to music director in 2009.

Paul Rardin joined the faculty of Temple University as director of choral activities in 2011. He conducts the Concert Choir, teaches graduate conducting, and oversees the six-choir program at Temple's Boyer College of Music and Dance. He previously taught at the University of Michigan and Towson University. Rardin's choral arrangements of spirituals and folk songs are published by Santa Barbara Music Publishing.

James Rodde is director of choral activities at Iowa State University, where he conducts the Iowa State Singers and the 130-voice Iowa Statesmen and teaches choral conducting and literature. His choirs have toured internationally and have appeared at ACDA, NCCO, and MENC national conventions. His choral editions appear in several publishers' catalogues.

Gary Schwartzhoff is professor of music and director of choral activities at the University of Wisconsin-Eau Claire, where he conducts Concert Choir, Chamber Choir, and The Singing Statesmen and teaches conducting. Schwartzhoff has presented choirs at twenty-four conventions before the state, divisional, and national levels of ACDA and MENC. He is also artistic director and conductor of The Master Singers, a community chamber ensemble with membership from throughout the Greater Chippewa Valley. Schwartzhoff serves as director of music at the First Congregational United Church of Christ in Eau Claire.

Ethan Sperry is director of choral activities at Portland State University and conductor of the Oregon Repertory Singers. Previously, he was a four-year member and assistant conductor of the Harvard Glee Club, and he taught at Miami University, where he directed the acclaimed Men's Glee Club. As composer and arranger, Sperry's work is performed internationally by both men's and mixed choirs. Sperry has served as the American Choral Directors Association's national chair of Repertoire and Standards for Male Choirs, as well as vice president of Intercollegiate Men's Choruses, Inc.

Robert Ward serves as director of choral activities at The Ohio State University, where he conducts the Men's Glee Club and Chorale. He also teaches graduate courses in conducting and choral literature. Prior to his appointment at Ohio State, Ward was for sixteen years a member of the music faculty at Oklahoma State University. He is the editor of a children's choral music series and a men's choral series published by Santa Barbara Music Publishers.

ABOUT THE AUTHOR

Jonathan Palant teaches at Richland College in Dallas, Texas, serves as minister of music at Dallas' Kessler Park United Methodist Church, and is the conductor of CREDO, an ecumenical mixed choir. Palant was artistic director of the Turtle Creek Chorale from 2007 to 2011. He has held collegiate teaching positions at Western Kentucky University and at Madonna University in Livonia, Michigan, and he taught secondary choral music at University School, an all-boys independent school in Cleveland, Ohio, and at San Pasqual High School in Escondido, California.

An active clinician and guest artist, Dr. Palant has conducted all-state men's choruses, presented interest sessions at regional and national music conventions, and been artist-in-residence both in the U.S. and in Canada. He has toured extensively with his choirs and led concert tours to Cuba, Denmark, England, Estonia, Finland, Italy, Latvia, Puerto Rico, Spain, and Sweden.

Dr. Palant sits on the board of directors of the Intercollegiate Men's Choruses and has served on the boards of the Michigan chapter of the American Choral Directors Association and of Youth First Texas, where he was founder and conductor of Dallas PUMP!, a choir serving at-risk youth.

Dr. Palant holds degrees from Michigan State University, Temple University, and the University of Michigan.